THE BEST OF
Birds&Blooms

contents

104

56

A Bucket List for Hummingbird Lovers

138

186

from the editor

What an incredible year!

For the editors at *Birds & Blooms* magazine it has been packed with amazing birding adventures and backyard discoveries. And 2015 gave us another special reason to celebrate—we turned 20! That's right—we've been in publication since 1995 and since then you have wowed us with your photos, stories and tips that grace the pages of our magazine.

Once again we're proud to offer you the most useful tips and secrets from readers and experts alike. Take your garden to the next level with the easy ideas in "A Dozen Ways to Dazzle" (page 132). Turn to "Top Songsters of America" (page 8) to find out which birds top our list of best singers and why you should keep your ears open for them in spring. And get creative with new ideas for unique containers in "Growing Outside the Box" (page 82).

Whether you're a gardener, birder or all-around nature lover, we hope *The Best of Birds & Blooms* provides inspiration as you continue to connect with the beauty in your backyard.

Stacy Tornio
Editor, *Birds & Blooms*

Never-Fail
Plants
(page 164)

EDITORIAL
Editor-In-Chief Catherine Cassidy
Creative Director Howard Greenberg
Editorial Operations Director Kerri Balliet

Managing Editor/Print & Digital Books Mark Hagen
Associate Creative Director Edwin Robles Jr.

Editor Amy Glander
Associate Editor Julie Kuczynski
Art Director Nancy Novak
Editorial Production Manager Dena Ahlers
Editorial Production Coordinator Jill Banks
Copy Chief Deb Warlaumont Mulvey
Copy Editor Mary-Liz Shaw
Editorial Services Administrator Marie Brannon
Editorial Business Manager Kristy Martin
Editorial Business Associate Samantha Lea Stoeger

Editor, *Birds & Blooms* Stacy Tornio
Associate Creative Director, *Birds & Blooms* Sharon K. Nelson
Senior Editor Kirsten Sweet
Associate Editor Kaitlin Stainbrook

BUSINESS
VP, Publisher Russell S. Ellis

TRUSTED MEDIA BRANDS, INC.
President & Chief Executive Officer Bonnie Kintzer
Chief Financial Officer/Chief Operating Officer Howard Halligan
Chief Revenue Officer Richard Sutton
Chief Marketing Officer Leslie Dukker Doty
Chief Digital Officer Vince Errico
Senior VP, Global HR & Communications
Phyllis E. Gebhardt, SPHR; SHRM-SCP
VP, Digital Content & Audience Development Diane Dragan
VP, Brand Marketing Beth Gorry
VP, Financial Planning & Analysis William Houston
Publishing Director, Books Debra Polansky
VP, Chief Technology Officer Aneel Tejwaney
VP, Consumer Marketing Planning Jim Woods

Pictured on the front cover:
Fritillary butterfly, Francis and Janice Bergquist
American robin, Bill Leaman

Pictured on the back cover:
Anna's hummingbird, Daniel Ferneding
Eastern tiger swallowtail on lantana, Paul D. Lemke/The Image Finders
Boat filled with flowers, Terry Wild Stock Inc.

CHAPTER 1

GEORGE GRALL/GETTY

the joys of Bird-Watching

Upgrade your birding skills with tips from the experts. Learn captivating details about some of North America's most abundant species, and share in the amazing experiences of bird-watching enthusiasts just like you.

Top Songsters in America

Discover the pleasures of listening to these expert nature singers.

BY SALLY ROTH

Song sparrow

And the winner is…the wood thrush. Or the hermit thrush. Or maybe it's the veery or the house finch. With hundreds of songbirds to choose from, picking the singer who reigns supreme depends on who's listening.

Whichever bird strikes a special chord in your heart, this list of soulful songsters will give you a few new favorites to keep an ear out for. Listen to some of the best.

American robin

Thrushes. Imagine yourself in a spring wood in the dim light at the end of the day, listening to the poignant song of a wood thrush. Pretty soon, you too may be inspired to write a love letter to this singer, as Thoreau did in his 1852 journal, extolling the wood thrush's evocation of "the liquid coolness of things drawn from the bottom of springs." The simple *ee-oh-lay* followed by a trill is haunting, no doubt, but it's the twilit surroundings that make it pure magic.

Another thrush with a delightful song is the veery. This bird's simple song, a whirling, reedy repetition of its own name, is delivered at dawn and dusk in the dim forest, going straight to the romantic heart of the listener.

The song of the hermit thrush isn't nearly as sweet and heart-tugging, but its rapid, liquid melody resonates because it follows some of our own musical scales, a trait that researchers only recently confirmed after carefully analyzing recordings.

Finally, a bird so common we tend to never give it a second glance: the American robin. Take a few minutes to listen, and you'll see it shares the musical talents of its thrush family.

Wrens. An unstoppable waterfall of notes spills from the throat of the tiny, indefatigable house wren, one of our most beloved backyard birds. Put up a birdhouse with a 1⅛-inch entrance, and you have a good chance of welcoming a whole family. The house wren is the virtuoso, but all wrens have voices that will make you smile.

Wood thrush

Winter wren

Orioles. Loud, clear, whistled songs are the hallmark of these vividly colored birds. Oranges, jelly and suet will bring them to your yard, but for a bit of extra temptation, put out a handful of string (6- to 10-inches long) for them to use during nest building.

Sparrows and finches. Every one of our native sparrows (more than two dozen species) has a song, and many are sweet and melodic. Listen for the common, brown-streaked song sparrow, which begins singing in late winter. House finches are among the earliest singers, beginning their complicated warbling not long after the turn of the year. Seeds are what all of these dozens of species prefer, so stock up on white proso millet for sparrows, sunflower seeds for finches and nyjer as a treat.

Mimic thrushes. Northern mockingbirds, gray catbirds and thrashers have charming songs, but they can imitate other sounds, too. You'll hear them singing at dawn, dusk and off and on throughout the day. They'll sometimes sing at night, too. The mockingbird in particular may take it to extremes, holding forth for hours from the rooftop right over your bed.

Grosbeaks. Less common than other songsters, the rose-breasted, black-headed and blue grosbeaks are all melodic warblers within their nesting ranges or along their spring migration routes. Once a rarity at feeders, they're becoming more and more frequent visitors. They'll eagerly eat sunflower seeds, as well as small, soft fruits from bushes or trees.

The most familiar grosbeak is one we don't usually think of, although its heavy bill says otherwise. It's the northern cardinal, one of our most abundant and beautiful backyard singers.

Tanagers. Seeing—or hearing—a tanager is usually a red-letter day because these birds aren't nearly as abundant as other songbirds. Still, keep your ears open for their long, robin-like songs, especially during spring migration, when they may stop off in any backyard. Some tanager songs have a hoarse quality, suggesting "a robin with a sore throat."

European starling. What's the scorned starling doing among the sweet-voiced beauties? Well, it's an incredible singer, too. Best of all, starlings begin singing in winter, just when it feels like spring will never come.

Bringing in the Singers

Insects and fruit are the natural menu for most of our finest songsters, including thrushes, orioles, tanagers, mimic thrushes and many grosbeaks. The more trees,

shrubs and other plants in your yard, the more of these birds you're likely to hear as they forage for insects and other natural food.

Many songbirds are only recently discovering feeders, so stock yours with a variety of offerings: Suet, mealworms, oranges, apples, peeled bananas and grapes are a great start. Don't hesitate to experiment, either. When I dumped small chunks of dried papaya in the feeder, a gray catbird and a Baltimore oriole took turns snatching them up. Orioles and a few others are famed for having a sweet tooth and will eat jams and jellies or visit a nectar feeder with perches. Finches, buntings, native sparrows and grosbeaks prefer seeds at the feeder. Another must is a birdbath. They're a big attraction for all songbirds.

The best way to find out who's singing and to learn the song is to use your own eyes and ears. Start with a bird you already know from your feeders. Get as close as you can to the singer; take a look using binoculars. Your patient study will be rewarded when you recognize the tune the next time you hear it.

Males do the singing in almost all species. Often, the songs are No Trespassing signs to other males, warning them that a nesting area has been claimed. Singing can also be a talent show meant to impress a female.

Summer tanager

Extraordinary Behaviors of Common Birds

Northern cardinals have a strong instinct to nurture young, like this male feeding juveniles.

It's always fun to identify backyard birds, but let's take it a step further and recognize the remarkable things our feathered friends are capable of. Looking beyond the basic facts makes our birding experience much richer. So here's a deeper dive into what makes birds such fascinating creatures!

BY LAURA ERICKSON

MARIE READ

Nature vs. Nurture

Eastern screech-owls are fierce little predators, unless their nurturing instinct gets in the way of their aggressive nature. In 1922, one observer reported that after a screech-owl's eggs were destroyed, it repeatedly entered a flicker nest for five days. The little owl brooded the nestling flickers and tried to feed them. Meanwhile, the parent flickers continued to provide proper care for their chicks.

Cardinals have a well-developed urge to nurture, too—or at least one in North Carolina did. Researchers speculate that a northern cardinal lost his young just when his hormonal drive to feed chicks was at its peak. He was carrying insects in his beak, searching for a cardinal chick to feed, when he discovered a goldfish on the edge of a backyard pool, its mouth roughly the size of a baby cardinal's—so he stuffed some food in. For several days he'd find a beakful of food, fly in and call from a nearby fence, and seven goldfish would crowd the edge of the pool to be fed. Pushing food into their mouths relieved his need to feed gaping orange mouths, and the goldfish apparently didn't object.

Internal Navigation

We know that migratory birds understand latitude, heading south in fall and north again in spring. But they also have a sense of where they are in terms of longitude. How do we know this? In the winter of 1961-'62, scientists performed an experiment with white-crowned and golden-crowned sparrows in the San Jose, California, area. Individuals of both species establish a wintering territory during their very first winter. Then they return to that spot faithfully, year after year.

The scientists captured and banded 411 of these sparrows and flew them by airplane to Baton Rouge, Louisiana, 1,800 miles southeast, for release. The next winter, 26 of them returned to San Jose. Next, the scientists captured 660 sparrows (including 22 of the birds that had already returned from Baton Rouge) and flew them to Laurel, Maryland, 2,400 miles east. The following winter, 15 of these birds returned to San Jose, including six individuals that had made the trip from Baton Rouge the previous year.

Adjusting to Low Temperatures

To survive winter, most birds grow lots of new feathers every fall. A female white-throated sparrow has about 1,500 feathers in October but over 2,700 in February. Those added feathers provide lots of insulation.

Besides adding feathers, though, birds such as black-capped chickadees turn down the thermostat. By day, a chickadee's body temperature is about 108 degrees. But on cold nights, that temperature can drop more than 20 degrees. First thing in the morning in winter, chickadees start shivering furiously. The muscle activity heats their

We know white-crowned sparrows have amazing internal navigation, thanks to a study done in

1961

The body temperature of black-capped chickadees can drop from a daytime high of 108 to a nighttime low of

88

body core back up to 108. Shivering requires additional energy, so chickadees must eat immediately to start their day. The chickadees that visit your yard at first light are counting on your feeders, but they have a backup just in case: They store food for times when favorite sources are depleted or bad weather keeps them away.

Remembering Food Sources

Chickadees, jays and other birds store food for when they need it most. How do they remember where they put it? Having an extraordinary spatial memory is only half the story.

Whether you're a human or a bird, every long-term memory is permanently stored on a neuron. Once a neuron holds a memory, it can't erase it to store a new memory. So why are chickadees masters at memorizing where they hide their seeds? Medical researchers and ornithologists have discovered that every autumn, neurons in a chickadee's brain die, to be replaced with new neurons. Wild chickadees, with a lot of worthless memories and a great need to store new ones, replace a great many neurons, while captive chickadees with lives that stay the same from day to day replace very few. Researchers hope that studying chickadee brains will help us figure out how to help humans with brain injuries or diseases.

Northern mockingbirds have a repertoire of about

200
songs.

White-throated sparrows need insulation in winter, so their feather count increases by **50%**

9 feet is a common width of eagles' nests because the birds add material to the same nest each year.

Forming Lifelong Bonds—Or Not

Most birds do not mate for life, and most of those that do aren't quite as faithful as we'd like to think. Over 92 percent of all bird species form a pair bond and stay together for at least part of the nesting cycle. Yet DNA tests of baby birds have shown that in over 75 percent of these species, some birds have mated with one or more birds other than their "social mate."

Some birds do bond for life, some for weeks or months. But with hummingbirds, it's only minutes! Males have no role in building a nest, incubating eggs or raising young.

On the other end of the spectrum are bald eagles. They mate for life, but possibly only because they can't work out a property settlement. Eagles don't stay together over winter, preferring separate vacations. The pair returns to the same nest each year, which can grow almost 9 feet wide. However, if one or the other doesn't come back, the remaining bird readily accepts a new mate at the nest.

Once you learn a bird's name, don't just check it off. Record when it arrives in spring, take note of the birds it hangs out with, watch its young grow, and observe how its behaviors change in different seasons. Looking for these habits will add another element of wonder to your backyard bird-watching.

Bird Facts by the Numbers

21%
A study found that black-capped chickadees took only about **21** percent of their daily energy from feeders.

100
While on the hunt for prey, eagles can dive up to **100** miles per hour. But in regular flight, they travel about **30** miles per hour.

40
Cowbirds may lay as many as **40** eggs per season.

31%
Common redpolls have **31** percent more plumage by weight in November than in July.

21,000
During their migration flight across the Atlantic Ocean, blackpoll warblers can reach heights of **21,000** feet.

THE *power*

While some people don't get into birds
until they retire, others start much younger.
Learn about a few extraordinary young birders.

BY KEN KEFFER

OF *Youth*

Just like these burrowing owl chicks, the birders featured on the next page are young, but mighty.

The beauty of bird-watching is that it appeals to people of all ages. Kids, especially, are full of curiosity, and birds can be captivating. It doesn't take much encouragement for this interest to become a lifelong hobby. There are flocks of incredible young birders out there. Here are a handful of them, along with their ideas for promoting conservation and encouraging fellow young birders.

▲ *Olivia Bouler*

15, Islip, New York

Interested in birds since she was 4 years old, Olivia was troubled by the news of the 2010 oil spill in the Gulf of Mexico. So she came up with a fundraising idea: giving bird drawings to people who contributed to wildlife recovery projects. Her initial goal was to give away 500 original drawings, and the response was incredible. Olivia helped raise more than $200,000 for organizations helping wildlife in the Gulf region. She received considerable recognition for her work, including being named an Audubon Artist Inspiring Conservation and a White House Champion of Change. In 2011, she wrote and illustrated *Olivia's Birds: Saving the Gulf* (Sterling Children's Books, $14.95). Olivia is currently writing and illustrating a graphic novel. She loves speaking to youth around the country about birds and saving their habitats. Olivia encourages all nature fans to take the time to learn more about conservation and birds.

▲ *The Martineau Family*

Elijah, 13; Brigham, 8; Nate, 17; Sariah, 11; May, 15, Lansing, Michigan

The Martineaus are a nature family. Backyard bird feeders and trips to Fenner Nature Center in their hometown were early inspirations for nature observation and study. They eventually joined both the Ohio Young Birders Club and Grand Rapids Junior Audubon. It's not uncommon for them to travel well over three hours to attend a birding event; interacting with peers and mentors in the natural world is a high priority for the family. The Martineau kids are active volunteers at a local bird-banding research station and at the Fenner Nature Center. They've often done science fair projects on birds, too. With interests in art and photography, Nate, May, Elijah and Sariah have all placed in the American Birding Association's Young Birder of the Year Contest for their outstanding field notebooks, sketches, writing and photography. Their enthusiasm for birds is winning over younger brother Brigham—and most everyone else who meets this family, too.

Landon Neumann ▶

17, Logansport, Indiana

Landon has been a birder since third grade, when he worked on a school assignment to put out feeders, and he has since become very involved at the local and state levels. He lives in an area that has relatively few birders, but he hasn't let that hinder his exploration. He likes to remind people that they don't have to travel to exotic locations to find birds. Last year he did a Big Year in his home county, spotting an impressive 220 species, many of which had never been documented there before! Trips throughout the U.S. and to Central America have boosted his life list to 815 species, but he is most proud of his efforts monitoring two purple martin colonies and a bluebird trail he started this year. Landon is also a big supporter of the Indiana Young Birders Club and has been a youth adviser for two years. He recently won the club's Young Birder of the Year Award.

▲ *Charlotte Wasylik*
17, Vermilion, Alberta

Charlotte's "spark bird" moment came six years ago when American goldfinches flocked to feeders her mother put up in their garden. Since then she's been photographing, sketching and writing about birds, which inspired her to start the Prairie Birder blog, *prairiebirder.wordpress.com*, to share her sightings and other experiences. That was in 2010; she founded the Alberta Birds Facebook group not long after. Although her parents aren't birders, they bought her books and found ways for her to connect with experienced birders. Charlotte believes it's important to let children experience nature when they're very young, so she works to introduce others to the natural world. She hosts a Young Naturalists' Corner at the Snow Goose Chase, an event that introduces immigrant and low-income families to nature in the province of Alberta. Charlotte was chosen to attend the Young Ornithologists' Workshop at Ontario's Long Point Bird Observatory in 2012; in 2013, she returned as an intern with an independent research project on the population decline of the monarch butterfly.

5 tips for encouraging young birders

Here's how to cultivate an interest in birds among the young people in your life.

Connect with peers. Many clubs for young birders are available from coast to coast. Seek out these organizations online; you'll find an outstanding network of active nature enthusiasts as well.

Legitimize the hobby. In an environment of endless practices, meetings and birthday parties, time spent in the natural world is often viewed as a luxury for children. Make nature a priority, and make time for sharing it with the kids close to you.

Diversify beyond birds. Growing up is a time for exploration. Encourage the young birders in your life to enjoy all aspects of nature. You don't have to know all the answers to facilitate curiosity and wonder.

Explore citizen science. A great way to engage young naturalists is with citizen science projects. Collecting data helps build focus and observation skills while also contributing to real science efforts. You can do this locally with nature organizations or even turn your data in online to groups like *ebird.org*.

Find career mentors. Many careers relate to the environment, and professionals will often be happy to share knowledge and offer job-shadowing opportunities to young adults. Investigate internships, too.

The *Titmouse*

Black-crested titmice

Tribe

A titmouse is a bird overflowing with sheer cuteness, complete with a cheery voice, perky crest and lots of energy. Five species of titmouse live in North America, and each of them is a popular backyard bird within its range. They're also coveted visitors to bird feeders and birdhouses. Here's a bit more about these spunky birds.

BY KENN AND KIMBERLY KAUFMAN

Tufted titmouse

Do you know which backyard songbird titmice are related to?

Same Family, Same Behavior

Titmice may not be as recognizable as chickadees, but they are related. It's easy to see the resemblance if you watch their behavior for a while. They have the same kind of active, acrobatic antics, flitting about the branches and hanging upside down from the ends of twigs as they search for insects. Like the chickadees, titmice are permanent residents, sticking around even during cold weather. Most are a little larger than chickadees, and they usually aren't as sociable, forming smaller flocks.

Popular in the East

The cheerful *peeto-peeto-peeto* song of the tufted titmouse can be heard all over the eastern half of the U.S., from Florida and eastern Texas to the Great Lakes and central New England. Most common in the South, titmice have been gradually extending their range northward in recent decades.

Members of a tufted titmouse pair may stay together all year, including in winter, when they're likely to join a mixed flock with chickadees, nuthatches and downy woodpeckers. In spring, the pair of titmice will leave the flock and find a suitable cavity for building their nest

and raising their young. The nest itself is a cup of leaves, moss, grass and bark strips, and lined with soft material, like animal hair. It isn't easy to find animal hair just lying around, though, and some daredevil titmice have been seen pulling hairs from sleeping dogs or cows!

Only the female incubates the eggs, but after the eggs hatch, the male does his share of feeding the young. And sometimes the pair of adults will have helpers. Their own young from the previous year may have stayed with the parents through the winter, and when that happens, they may stick around to help feed their younger siblings in the new nest.

Texas Resident

Walk into a riverside forest in southern Texas and you may think you're hearing the song of a tufted titmouse, but when the bird pops out into the open, you'll see that it has a white forehead and a striking black crest. Once considered to belong to the same species as the tufted titmouse, it is now classified as a separate species: the black-crested titmouse. It's widespread and common in southern and central Texas, extending south into eastern Mexico and north into the edge of southwestern Oklahoma. In

CATHY & GORDON ILLG; STEVE AND DAVE MASLOWSKI (2):

Bridled titmouse

Titmice or Titmouses?

Some purists insist that the plural should be "titmouses"—they point out that these birds have no connection to the little rodents called mice. But they've been known as "titmice" for so long that either name will do!

its song, call notes and behavior, it is very much like its tufted cousin.

In east-central Texas, the black-crested titmouse sometimes interbreeds with the tufted titmouse. The resulting hybrids usually have dark gray crests, and a spot of reddish brown on the forehead.

A Drab and Delightful Duo

Across the western states you may notice plain gray titmice with short, pointed crests and no trace of any brighter color or pattern. They might look dull at first glance, but watch for a while and you'll discover that they are spunky, active little birds, brimming with personality.

For many years, these were regarded as just one species under the appropriate name of plain titmouse. But in the 1990s, studies proved that they were actually two separate species, with different voices and different choices of habitat. So now we have the oak titmouse living in the oak woods of California and extreme southern Oregon, and the juniper titmouse inhabiting woods of juniper and pinyon pine in the interior of the west, from northeastern California to New Mexico.

The oak titmouse is a common visitor to backyard bird

Suet, seeds and a nest box will attract titmice to your backyard.

Black-crested titmouse

23

Juniper titmouse

Oak titmouse

feeders along parts of the California coast. Compared to other titmice, it seems less sociable. Pairs may wander through the woods together, but they don't usually join up with bigger flocks.

Juniper titmice are sometimes hard to find. In arid, open woods of juniper and pinyon pine, they live in scattered pairs and small flocks. But in the Southwest, they will sometimes join up with flocks of their sharp-looking relative, the bridled titmouse.

A Southwestern Specialty

In the mountains of Arizona and New Mexico, in the woodlands of canyons and foothills, flocks of bridled titmice flit through the oaks. These are the smallest of the titmice, and they often seem to sound and act more like chickadees. But in addition to the bridle-like face pattern that gives them their name, they have the sharp, pointed crest of a typical titmouse.

More than other titmice, this one loves company. They break up into pairs for the nesting season, but at other times of year, bridled titmice may travel in flocks of 20 or more.

Small in stature but big on personality, all of these titmice liven up their surroundings in a particularly endearing fashion. Be sure to watch and listen for them on your next bird walk and follow our tips for enticing them to your yard, too.

Attracting Titmice to your Backyard

If you live in the range of one of these titmouse species, it's not hard to lure them to your yard. Here are some basics to bring them in.

MATURE TREES. This is the main requirement: Titmice won't live in treeless terrain. Tufted and black-crested titmice favor tall, deciduous trees, while the names of oak and juniper titmice give clues about their preferences. But wherever you are, some good-sized trees native to your own region are great choices.

SUNFLOWER SEEDS. These popular seeds, especially the black-oil variety of sunflower seeds, are magnets for titmice. In fall and winter, titmice may make dozens of trips from your feeder to nearby trees, carrying away one sunflower seed at a time to hide it in a tree crevice or under bark.

SUET AND SUBSTITUTES. In the wild, titmice eat both seeds and insects. At the feeder, complement the seeds by offering raw suet, suet cakes or some other protein source like peanut butter mixtures.

NEST BOXES. Titmice aren't attracted to artificial nesting sites as readily as some other birds, but they will use a nest box designed for bluebirds, especially if it's placed a little higher—perhaps 8 to 10 feet off the ground—in a shady location.

bird tales

Our readers share some of their best birding stories.

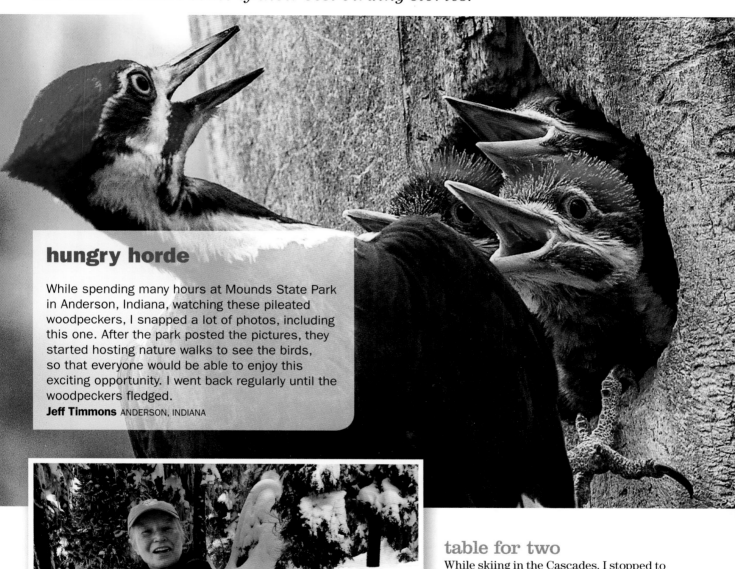

hungry horde

While spending many hours at Mounds State Park in Anderson, Indiana, watching these pileated woodpeckers, I snapped a lot of photos, including this one. After the park posted the pictures, they started hosting nature walks to see the birds, so that everyone would be able to enjoy this exciting opportunity. I went back regularly until the woodpeckers fledged.

Jeff Timmons ANDERSON, INDIANA

table for two

While skiing in the Cascades, I stopped to eat and quickly made a feathered friend. This gray jay was right at home sharing my lunch.

Chris Shuraleff EUGENE, OREGON

BACKYARD TIP Gray jays are curious birds that eat just about anything and are often fearless around humans if offered a handout.

bird tales

redbird row

With a heavy blanket, tripod, Canon SLR camera and hot cocoa, I'll layer up, open my sliding glass door and wait by the feeders for a photo. We had a terrible blizzard in January 2013, and I shot hundreds of photos until it was too dark. I got some amazing lineups on the fence.

Carol Estes LA PORTE, INDIANA

Blossom Thief

I photographed this house finch at the Horticultural Center in Philadelphia. The bird dropped the cherry blossom out of its mouth shortly after I snapped the shutter.

Jill Achanzar ATCO, NEW JERSEY

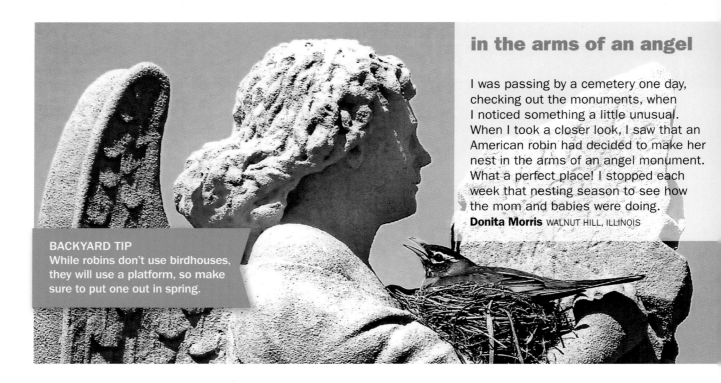

in the arms of an angel

I was passing by a cemetery one day, checking out the monuments, when I noticed something a little unusual. When I took a closer look, I saw that an American robin had decided to make her nest in the arms of an angel monument. What a perfect place! I stopped each week that nesting season to see how the mom and babies were doing.

Donita Morris WALNUT HILL, ILLINOIS

BACKYARD TIP
While robins don't use birdhouses, they will use a platform, so make sure to put one out in spring.

seeing double

Near the end of June, I became aware of a strange sound coming from the woods behind our house. Through the Cornell Lab of Ornithology website, *allaboutbirds.org*, I learned the sound I was hearing belonged to fledgling barred owls begging for food. The next day, I located three young barred owls perched high in the trees along with an adult owl.

Over the next several weeks, I found the owlets at various locations in our woods by listening for their begging calls. Two of the owlets seemed inseparable, always located on the same branch, snuggled close together. This photo was taken on one such encounter, with the two owlets looking back over their shoulders at me.

Dorrie Holmes GRANVILLE, MASSACHUSETTS

Great Catch!

On my weekly lunch date with my wife, I saw a flock of cedar waxwings in the crab apple trees. This one picked a berry, flipped it up and swallowed it. It was a good catch, and I had a good catch of my own—capturing this photo in mid-flip. These birds were great fun to watch and photograph.

George Hernandez Jr. BOISE, IDAHO

DID YOU KNOW?
Every once in a while, the tip of a waxwing's tail is orange instead of yellow. This is based on diet.

Follow My Lead

Every day for three months, a sandhill crane family performed a funny ritual behind my house. One of the adults would lead its chick into the pond water and swim to the island. Upon arrival, there would be much wing flapping. In this photo, the youngster seems to be mimicking the adult with its tiny, half-formed wings.

Allen Bosch VENICE, FLORIDA

bluebird of happiness

Feeling a little down, I set out on a hike one morning to lift my spirits. I heard this male eastern bluebird before I saw him. He landed on a branch and stayed long enough for me to get a photo. Instantly, my blues were banished, and I smiled as I walked back down the trail.

Dave Weth NORMAL, ILLINOIS

The most common birds of
NORTH AMERICA

A look at the continent's most abundant
birds and why they are true survivalists.

BY KENN AND KIMBERLY KAUFMAN

Red-winged blackbirds

Yellow-rumped warbler

You often hear about rare birds. People who are involved in conservation spend a lot of time thinking about them, and that's certainly true for the two of us. We're big advocates for whooping cranes, with only about 400 left in the world. Another species we often talk about is the Kirtland's warbler, which was down to about 300 just a few years ago.

Rare birds tend to be rare for a reason. The Kirtland's, for example, has a highly specialized habitat. It will raise its young only in large groves of short, young jack pine trees growing on sandy soil in just a few parts of Michigan and nearby areas.

While such rare species certainly deserve attention and care, what about their opposites? You know—those birds that seem to be everywhere!

Often these birds are successful because they're generalists. Unlike the Kirtland's warbler, they don't have specialized habitats—they can make do just about anywhere. Here's a look at these easygoing birds and the qualities that make them so abundant.

Red-winged Blackbird

Male red-wings, flashing their scarlet shoulder patches, are a familiar sight all over North America. While some marsh birds have become rare, red-wings don't need pristine marshes. They'll adapt to any pond edge, weedy ditch or even brushy field. There are probably some red-wings nesting in just about every county in the Lower 48 states, with a population estimated at 130 million to 190 million.

Yellow-rumped Warbler

Tiny, colorful warblers are often hard to see as they flit from treetop to treetop, but they can swarm through the woods in great numbers during spring and fall migration. North America boasts more than 50 species of warblers; this one is probably the most abundant. It comes in two varieties, with the white-throated "Myrtle" type nesting from New England to Alaska and the yellow-throated "Audubon's" all over the

forests and mountains of the West. More adaptable than most warblers, these yellow-rumps eat berries as well as insects, so they can survive cold weather without migrating to the tropics. Their total population may be as high as 130 million.

Mourning Dove

Adapted to a variety of open habitats, these doves also raise a lot of youngsters—as many as six broods a year in warmer climates. So even though they ordinarily lay only two eggs per clutch, a pair can produce up to a dozen offspring every year. Estimates of their population range as low as 100 million and as high as 475 million.

Dark-eyed Junco

If you see lots of juncos around your feeders in winter, you're not alone. These little snowbirds are thought to be among the most numerous North American species, with estimates of

Mourning doves

American robin

Are Estimates Accurate?

The numbers cited by experts on bird populations vary greatly. Mourning doves, for instance, are thought to number between a low of 100 million and a high of 475 million—almost five times the lowest estimate—but no one can be sure. Even the most highly trained ornithologists and conservationists can only make educated guesses.

Dark-eyed junco

150 million, 200 million or even more. Although they nest only in the North Woods and the mountains, they're among the most common summer birds all across the vast forested regions of Canada, Alaska and the Northern states.

American Robin

Originally they inhabited forests and swamps, but robins quickly learned to live around towns and cities when settlers began clearing the land. Today robins are abundant in towns, city parks, farms and forests. They nest all across Canada and Alaska, and in most parts of the Lower 48 states, except for the hottest Southern regions. Their total population has been estimated at 300 million.

European Starling

Brought to this continent around 1890 and released in Central Park, starlings have been wildly successful. Their total numbers here are above 50 million; some estimate that they may top 200 million. Starlings are smart, adaptable and tough, so their success isn't surprising. Unfortunately, they've thrived at the expense of some native birds, taking over nesting sites of woodpeckers, bluebirds and others.

Mallard

We know more about duck numbers than we do about populations of most birds, because wildlife agencies keep careful counts of them every year. We know, for instance, that the North American mallard population in 2014 is around 11 million—higher than the long-term average, which is just under 8 million. Of course, that total number is much lower than the estimates for some of the songbirds. But ducks are big birds, and a million mallards take up a lot more room than a million robins.

Ducks are big birds, and a million mallards take up a lot more room than a million robins.

Chipping sparrow

Chipping Sparrow

When European settlers began building towns and cities in eastern North America, tiny, tame chipping sparrows were among the first native birds to move in. They might have become the reigning city sparrows of this continent if house sparrows hadn't been introduced from Europe; the bigger, more aggressive house sparrows took over the more populous areas. But chipping sparrows are still extremely common in suburbs, farms and open woods, with some experts putting their population at more than 200 million.

Red-eyed Vireo

Bird-watchers are often surprised to learn that these vireos are among the continent's most common birds.

Swainson's thrush

Red-eyed vireo

Moving slowly among the dense foliage of treetops, they're very hard to see. But as soon as you learn to recognize their voice, you'll discover that they're indeed abundant. Their numbers may be overestimated because they're such tireless singers, continuing to deliver their short, melodic phrases through the hot summer when many other birds have fallen silent. Even so, their population is probably over 80 million and perhaps more than 130 million.

Swainson's Thrush

Stand outside on a clear night in spring or fall, and you may hear the soft, musical notes of these thrushes high overhead, migrating in the dark. These shy brown birds are thought to be among the continent's most abundant, with estimates as high as 100 million. The key to their success is their vast breeding range, throughout the boreal forests of Canada and Alaska, as well as the Northeastern states and all the higher mountains of the West.

3 Ways to Help Count the Birds

By taking part in any of these projects, you'll help provide data that scientists can use to track bird population trends.

1. Christmas Bird Count. This annual winter census by the National Audubon Society has gone on every year since 1900. Even if you're a new birder, you can take part in the count by teaming up with experienced observers between mid December and early January. To find a local count and specific dates, see *birds.audubon.org*.

2. Project FeederWatch. From early November through about the end of March, volunteers do regular counts at backyard feeders, turning in the results to the Cornell Lab of Ornithology. You'll find more information at *feederwatch.org*.

3. Great Backyard Bird Count. A cooperative project of Audubon and Cornell, this count takes place over four days in February. Despite the name, it isn't limited to backyards; you can count birds anywhere and submit the results. Visit *gbbc.birdcount.org* to find more information and specific dates.

beyond
Flight

Gain a new appreciation fo

Close-up of blue jay feathers

the power of feathers.

BY KENN AND KIMBERLY KAUFMAN

The gorgeous red plumage of a cardinal or the vivid blue of a blue jay can make us stop in our tracks with their beauty. Feathers are among the things that make birds so special and no other creature in the animal kingdom has them. But feathers don't just look pretty—they perform some very important jobs, too.

Painted bunting

Structure

Feathers are among nature's most remarkable structures. A typical feather has a narrow shaft running through the center and a flat vane on either side. The vanes are made up of thin barbs, and each barb has tiny branches called barbules, which often have microscopic hooks along the edges. If the barbs are separated, they can be zipped together again, with the tiny hooks holding them together to form a thin but strong surface.

Underneath this outer layer, there's usually a layer of down feathers. These feathers lack the tiny hooks that hold the barbs together, so they're very soft and loose.

Thermoregulation

Thermoregulation is a bird's ability to keep itself at a comfortable temperature. Feathers act as insulation against the cold and heat. The number of feathers on a bird varies with the season, and a bird will typically have more feathers during the winter months. Birds can also fluff out their feathers to hold in even more heat. In lower temperatures, the muscles below the skin automatically contract, just as ours do when we get goose bumps. The contracting muscles raise the feathers, which creates more air space between the feathers and skin, and traps warm air in the plumage.

Between the bird's skin and the outer coating of visible feathers is the layer of soft down feathers. Anyone who wears a down jacket or sleeps under a down comforter knows the insulating power of these feathers. Some birds take advantage of this built-in insulation and use it in their nests. Female eider ducks pluck some of their own down feathers to line their nests, creating a cozy, insulated layer around their eggs.

Decoration

Colorful feathers are one of the reasons birds are so popular. Of course, birds don't wear those beautiful hues for us, but for each other.

Male birds with the brightest colors or fanciest plumage often have the best chance of attracting a mate and defending a nesting territory against other males.

Some feathers even have decorations invisible to us. Unlike humans, most birds can see ultraviolet colors, and studies have shown that many birds have

Fun feather fact

A small songbird has fewer than 4,000 feathers. A swan might have as many as 25,000.

Anna's hummingbird

Fun feather fact

Hummingbirds beat their wings about 60 times per second, creating a soft buzzing sound.

Wood duck males have bright and beautiful plumage, but they are elusive. They like to hide deep in the thickets of ponds and rivers.

distinctive ultraviolet plumage patterns. In some species, in which the males and females look the same to us, birds tell each other apart by the different patterns of ultraviolet light reflected from their feathers.

Camouflage

Birds are sometimes safer if they can avoid being seen, and many have feathers with camouflage patterns, which can range from simple, drab colors to elaborate stripes and lines. A striped savannah sparrow can almost disappear in the dry grass of a field or marsh. And a ruffed grouse has feathers with a speckled, mottled pattern to disguise it in the dappled light of the forest undergrowth—but only when it's not in display, like the one on the opposite page.

Sound Production

Feathers of certain shapes, moving rapidly through the air, make noticeable sounds. Sometimes the results seem coincidental, like the whistling made by the wings of a mourning dove when it takes off. But some birds have highly modified feathers that create very distinctive notes, which they incorporate into musical aerial displays.

The American woodcock is a chunky bird that can be found in eastern forests and damp fields. On spring nights, the male performs a flight display, flying high in the air and then spiraling down with a twittering, chippering sound. Oddly enough, this twittering isn't a vocal noise—the vibrations of the wings' outer feathers produce it. Similarly,

a Wilson's snipe makes a winnowing sound with its narrow tail feathers, and hummingbirds "hum" by the rapid beating of their wings.

Sound Suppression

Conversely, the feathers of some birds are very effective at muffling sounds. Owls, which have the remarkable ability to fly with silent wingbeats, are a great example. Although most birds have large flight feathers that are strong and stiff, owls' flight feathers have soft, loose edges, deadening the sound when their wings cut through the air.

Fishing owls are the exception. As tropical predators that swoop down to catch fish in streams and rivers, these owls lack softened flight feathers. They don't need them because the fish

Fun feather fact

Birds molt and replace their feathers at least once per year.

Ruffed grouse

Wilson's snipe

Owls, like this short-eared owl, can sneak up on their prey because they have feathers that help them have a silent flight.

Fun feather fact

The feathers of a bald eagle weigh more than twice as much as its skeleton.

are under the water and can't hear them.

The next time you find yourself admiring the beautiful feathers or colors of a bird, take a closer look. You might be surprised by what you find.

Bald eagle

SUNSET BIRDING

▸▸ Don't stop bird-watching when the sun goes down.
For some species, things are just getting started.

BY KEN KEFFER

The early bird might catch the worm, but that doesn't mean you have to be up at dawn to enjoy bird-watching. You can find birds throughout the day—sunup to sundown— and into the night. Not only can evening be the best time to catch certain species, but it's also a great opportunity to be outside. Gorgeous sunsets are a bonus.

The Evening Chorus

While not as boisterous as the dawn chorus, there is a flurry of bird activity as the day turns to night. Much like in the morning, the American robin will probably be the merriest of songsters in the evening. Its *cheery-up, cheery-oh* call is more welcome at sunset (at least for me), than it is during the predawn hour.

Birds aren't the only evening callers. Listen for frogs and toads, and remember they don't just *ribbit* or *croak*. Toads are especially noisy as the sun is setting. Their steady trilling is the background noise to many summer evenings.

Nightfall is the time for flying mammals, too. Bats can be spotted fluttering in the twilight hours as they feed on insects. Their silent and erratic flight is mesmerizing. As it gets dark, they can be hard to see. Try looking at city streetlights or over country ponds that offer a little glow for your best chance at spotting them.

Owl Prowls

Sunset is when most owls are just waking up for their nocturnal rounds, so it's a fantastic time to go on an owl walk. In many areas you can hear owls throughout the year, but late winter is an especially active period since it's breeding season for several species. Late summer is also great for owl fans because little owlets are testing their vocal chords for the first time.

You need to know what you're listening for, though. For example, great horned owls have a classic hoot. Males and females will sometimes even hoot in unison, with the females giving a higher pitch hoot than males. Not all owls hoot, however.

Screech-owls are widespread with three species found

Eastern screech-owls let out a wailing sound that is reminiscent of a horse whinny.

Go on an evening owl prowl to see barred owls.

Wilson's snipe often head out to feed around dusk.

Listen for the woodcock's *peent* calls at dusk.

throughout the U.S. Maybe you've heard their calls and never realized it. They make various sounds, including toots, trills and a wailing reminiscent of a horse whinny.

While less widespread, barred owls can be locally abundant in the eastern U.S., across Canada, and into the Pacific Northwest. They have a highly recognizable *who-cooks-for-you* call. You can listen to it and the screech-owl at *allaboutbirds.org*.

Sky Dancers

A classic evening bird tradition is that of the American woodcock's sky dance. Woodcocks are portly shorebirds more at home in the upland woods than along the edge of the water. On spring evenings, males perform an elaborate territorial display in open areas adjacent to woods. They

A nighthawk's *pzeent* call sounds similar to a woodcock's.

sit on the ground making their repetitive *peent* call. Then they explode skyward, their wings making a twittering flutter. They circle higher and higher before plummeting back to the ground. Then they repeat the entire process.

A bird related to the woodcock is the Wilson's snipe. This shorebird also makes aerial flight displays as the sun goes down. The winnowing of the snipe has a hollow, haunting sound. The noise of the snipe is created by air flowing over their tail. Wilson's snipe are widespread across the continent. Look for them in open wet areas, especially damp fields and marshy pond edges.

Sunsets with Swifts

Historically, chimney swifts would roost in hollow trees, in caves and along cliffs, but these days, they are almost entirely dependent on human structures for their nighttime needs. After soaring around all day searching for flying insects to eat, swifts congregate in communal roosts, often in smokestacks and chimneys. You can watch as thousands of them fly into the structures at dusk, most notably during migration. In recent years the chimney swift has been declining as these open roosting sites become less common. In some instances artificial chimney swift towers have been installed to help the population.

The chimney swift is an eastern bird, but other similar species can be found in the West. They are less likely to roost in human structures, but that doesn't mean they are any less impressive to see. For instance, the white-throated swift is a western bird found in mountains and canyons, and the Vaux's swift resides in the Pacific Northwest.

Nightjars

The nightjars include nighthawks, whip-poor-wills and their relatives. This group is sometimes referred to as goatsuckers, based on the myth that they come out at night to nurse from goats. Instead, this nocturnal group with ridiculously wide mouths feeds on flying insects they scoop out of the air.

Many, like the eastern whip-poor-will and chuck-will's-widow, are named after their loud and repetitive calls. The *whip-poor-will* has added emphasis on the first and third syllable, while the *chuck-will's-widow* is softest on the initial note.

Despite their name, you can occasionally see common nighthawks foraging during the day. They're most active at night, though. Nighthawks have long, slender wings and a seemingly erratic flight pattern. You'll be alerted to their presence by hearing a *pzeent* call that sounds similar to a woodcock's. Watch closely as they zip and dart around, catching flying insects.

The dawn chorus can be a sight and a sound to behold, but give evening birding a try. You won't be disappointed. From owls to woodcocks, and from swifts to nighthawks, there is a lot to see. And the best part is you don't have to wake up early to catch the action.

that's not a duck

BY KEN KEFFER

Purple gallinule

If it looks like a duck and acts like a duck, then it must be a duck, right? Think again! There are a number of bird species often confused with ducks, but they aren't actually related at all. Let's take a look at some of these duck doppelgängers to set the record straight.

American Coot

American coots are related to rails. If you get a good look at this black water bird, notice the white, chicken-like bill and frontal shield. It also has partially lobed toes, not webbed feet like a duck's. Coots are often seen swimming together in large numbers.

I've affectionately dubbed its unique swimming and head bobbing action the "coot scoot." Hesitant to take flight, coots will flap frantically as they scurry along the water's surface.

Common Gallinule

A close relative of the coot's, the common gallinule (formerly common moorhen) is prevalent in the southern coastal states. Look for the noticeable red bill and frontal shield on adult common gallinules.

Gallinules can resemble ducks when they swim, but they also have an impressive habit of walking on water

American coot

American coot

(or rather, walking on floating vegetation). Gallinules have huge feet with remarkably long toes. The young chicks even have specialized spurs or hooks on their wings to help them grab and climb along their nests. Similar to the common gallinule, look for the purple gallinule in the southeast with rich purples, blues, greens, yellows and reds.

Pied-billed Grebe

Pied-billed grebes make some interesting noises, including wailing *whoops* and *kuhs*, but you'll never hear one quack. Pied-billed are the most widespread of the North American grebes. Grebes have lobed toes and are most comfortable in the water. Their legs are back on the body, making walking a difficult task.

Instead of taking flight, grebes will often dive when they feel threatened. Some species, including the pied-billed, can also adjust their buoyancy and will sink down like a submarine, swimming along with just their heads sticking up like a periscope.

Pied-billed grebe

Eared grebe

It's a Quack

Quack, quack. Even though we think of it as a typical duck call, only a few, including the female mallard, actually quack.

Eared Grebe

During the breeding season, eared grebes sport yellow tufts of feathers along the sides of the head. In nonbreeding plumage, these birds are slate gray with accents of black and white, resembling both horned and pied-billed grebes.

Like other grebes, the eared grebe chicks will ride atop the backs of their parents. They can even remain in place as the adults dive underwater. Adults will eat feathers and feed them to their young. This is to filter fish bones and crustacean bits in the stomach. When staging for migration, eared grebes will congregate in large numbers at Utah's Great Salt Lake and California's Mono Lake.

Double-crested Cormorant

Like the mergansers they resemble, double-crested cormorants are fish eaters. But unlike mergansers, cormorants aren't ducks. You might see them swimming low in the water, but you are just as likely to spot one basking in the sun with its wings spread wide. They don't

Double-crested cormorant

have nearly as much preening oil as ducks, so cormorants air-dry their feathers.

Once you learn the distinctive long-tailed and long-necked shape of the cormorant, they're easy to pick out, even in flight. Their namesake double-crests are only visible during the breeding season, and even then, they can be subtle and hard to see.

Common Loon

The common loon has a haunting, almost yodel-like sound, which echoes across the northern lakes it frequents in the summer. Males and females have the same beautiful summer colors, which includes a dark red eye, jet-black head and bold, black-and-white pattern across the back and chest.

Loons definitely have a duck-like shape, though their bills are long and sharp, perfect for diving down to find fish. While most think of loons as summer birds, you can often spot them in the winter (though their plumage has faded) all over the coasts of North America. If you're looking for common loons along the coast in winter, keep an eye out for the red-throated and Pacific species, too.

Whistling-duck

How can this not be a duck? It even has duck in the name. Both the black-bellied and the fulvous whistling-ducks are more closely related to swans and geese than to true ducks. Look for them in the southern states, especially Arizona, Texas and Florida, although they can wander farther to the north.

Male and female whistling-ducks look the same, and both help raise the whistling-ducklings. Fulvous whistling-ducks will nest on the ground, while black-bellied will use nest boxes placed near or over water. They can be quite conspicuous within their limited ranges.

Black-bellied whistling-duck

Water Birds

These are all water birds, but not waterfowl. That term only applies to the duck family, including geese and swans.

Common loon

glad you asked!

Kenn and Kimberly Kaufman answer your birding questions.

Q&A

DID YOU KNOW?
You often see orioles feeding on oranges and grape jelly, but they also eat insects.

The only time I see Baltimore orioles in my yard is in spring when the apple trees are blooming. They appear to be destroying the blossoms. Are they after the nectar?
Douglas Cestone Glen Rock, New Jersey
Kenn and Kimberly: You're right—orioles are big fans of nectar. Among North American birds, they are second only to hummingbirds as frequent flower visitors. In their zeal to get at the nectar, orioles do sometimes destroy blossoms, but in other cases, they have been proven to be effective pollinators.

◄I live on the Au Sable, a fast-moving river. Quite often, a great blue heron is seen fishing off my front porch. Do male and female herons look the same? Also, why do I never see a pair of them?
Marjorie Roper GRAYLING, MICHIGAN
Kenn and Kimberly: With great blue herons, the male and female look almost exactly alike. On average, males are a little larger with longer ornamental plumes, but these distinctions are so slight and variable that it's hard to see the difference, even when members of a pair are together. And the members of a pair are together only when they are at the nest. That's where they do all their courtship and all their interactions around raising their young. When they fly off to find food for themselves or their young, they go separately, not as a pair.

It's been stated that birds have no sense of smell or taste. So why do most species prefer certain seeds?
Betty Robinson WEST BRANCH, MICHIGAN
Kenn and Kimberly: Birds actually do have some sense of taste. It's not well developed in most species, as evidenced by the use of cayenne pepper in birdseed to discourage squirrels. The question of whether birds can smell needs more study. We do know that some have a highly developed sense of smell. Turkey vultures, for example, have a keen sense of smell, helping them locate the carrion they feed on. It's more likely seed-savvy birds are making selections based on what seeds suit the shape of their bill, and following their instincts for nutritional value and seed quality.

I have lots of woodpeckers at my feeders, and I frequently see hairies and downies arrive together. Is it a coincidence, or do these two birds mingle?

Lori Patrouille GILMAN, WISCONSIN

Kenn and Kimberly: The answer depends on the time of year. In winter, downy and hairy woodpeckers often travel in mixed flocks with other woodland birds. When they're hanging out with the same crowd, there's a good chance they'll arrive at your feeders together. At other times of the year, while they often share the same habitats, they don't travel in flocks. So in warmer weather, when they arrive together, it's probably pure coincidence.

We live in a rural area and have problems with mockingbirds attacking other birds that come into the yard. Can you suggest a way to discourage them?

Donny and Lavone Leggett
HAZLEHURST, GEORGIA

Kenn and Kimberly: Mockingbirds are naturally aggressive, and it's a challenge to keep them from dominating other birds. One possible approach is to rearrange things in your yard. Mockingbirds are most defensive around the location of their nest and some prime food sources, which would include certain fruiting shrubs. If your feeders are currently close to bushes where the mockingbirds build their nest, or close to plants with berries that they like, you may be able to keep the peace in your yard by moving the feeders farther away from these areas of conflict.

▶ I clean my birdbaths many times during the summer, but it seems like they're not actually getting clean. What's the proper way to do this?

Janice Ruesch FAIRPORT, NEW YORK

Kenn and Kimberly: Depending on the material your bath is made from, a mixture of water and bleach can be an effective cleaning solution. If you're in doubt about how well the material of your bath will hold up to this mixture, be sure to test a small area first. If the bath is made of concrete, empty it out, and using a hose with a high-pressure nozzle, spray off any built-up algae or dirt. Add water to the bath until it's almost full, and then add 1 to 1½ cups of bleach. Cover the entire bath with a black plastic trash bag to prevent any birds from getting to the bleach water,

DID YOU KNOW?
Changing the water in your birdbath every few days will help keep algae from growing, making it easier to clean in the long run.

and allow it to soak for 10-15 minutes. Remove the plastic bag, carefully drain the bleach water mix in a safe area, and rinse the bath thoroughly for a few minutes until you can no longer detect the smell of bleach.

FAQ

66It seems our birds (and squirrels) feed on a schedule. They all come to the feeders at the same time and stop feeding at the same time. Why does this happen?99
ED AND CAROLE AMSBURY GAINESVILLE, FLORIDA

Kenn and Kimberly: Most feeder birds are sociable creatures. Often they travel in mixed flocks, arriving and departing together. Even if they're not with a flock, birds pay attention to what other birds are doing. If several are already at your feeders, others will know it's safe to visit. Then, if something alarms the birds and a few fly away, most of the others will fly off, too. They'll watch from a distance until the first brave birds come back, and then others will return. Another explanation is that they may all just go off to another neighborhood for a while. As for the squirrels, they also pay attention to what the birds are doing, taking advantage of all those watchful eyes to help them avoid danger.

Painted buntings

BIRDING *on the*

They take bird-watching to work, creating a powerful ripple effect

Kelly works with her class on bird identification.

JOB

wherever they go.

In the Classroom

My name is Kelly Preheim, and I'm a kindergarten teacher in Armour, South Dakota. Four years ago, I went to my first bird festival and it changed my life.

As I kept learning more and more about birds, I started talking to my elementary school students about them. They were fascinated, asking about habitat, behavior, migration and even bird songs. I had one little boy often say to me, "What else you got?"

Now I incorporate birds almost on a daily basis into our regular lessons, and it's amazing what the kids absorb. One year, I had a group of students learn to identify more than 400 birds by sight and 100 birds by song. They especially loved owls and raptors.

By teaching kids about birds, I've seen their self-confidence soar. These kids love knowing something that most adults know little about.

I know the kids are only 5 and 6, but they are capable of learning so much. As they grow more confident in birds, I see it trickle into other subjects. They are also aware of what's going on outdoors, becoming lifelong learners and stewards of their environment.

When people ask me why I do this, I think about the ripple effect. I see young children learning from me, and in turn, teaching their families and friends. Then these families embrace their young birders, buying them bird books, flash cards, puzzles, bird toys, and best of all, taking them on outings to look at birds. Families are finding that birding and being out in nature is inexpensive, and the quality time spent with a child creates memories to last a lifetime.

MARK VANDERWERFF

No matter what your job is, sometimes all it takes is a quick break to get refueled and rejuvenated.

Kelly takes her kindergarten students outside to explore.

On the Job Site

My name is Patrick Hogan, and I started birding on the job a couple of years ago. It's OK—my boss knows. I live in Temperance, Michigan, and work for Terra Probe Environmental as a utility locator and drill rig operator. I'm outside most of the time, in locations all over the Midwest. From one day to the next, I can go from an overgrown industrial site with a couple of hundred acres to an active gas station in an urban area. And believe it or not, I look forward to seeing birds in both places.

I've never been one to only get caught up in rare bird sightings. From the peregrine falcon I spotted in downtown Detroit to my first northern mockingbird on the Ohio River, I enjoy them all. In particular, I really love seeing birds in urban areas. I expect to see something fun in large, overgrown lots that are heavily wooded, but when there's nothing green around and then a cool bird shows up, it's a great surprise.

My job can be mentally and physically demanding, so it's important to have something to help keep my sanity and break up the day a bit. For me, this escape is birding. After I get my tasks done on a particular job, it's nice to

relax for a minute or two and notice the natural world around me. Lately, I've even been getting my co-workers and other contractors involved. When we have our tailgate meetings on a job site, they'll often ask me what I've been seeing or they want to show me a picture of something they saw themselves.

Golfing, working, hunting, fishing, doing yard work—I bird everywhere I go. I like to tell people that it's the best passive hobby there is. I hope others I talk to about birding spread it to a few people they know, too. If people can connect with nature, they will appreciate it. And if they appreciate it, they will protect it.

In the Service

My name is Bobbie Ragsdale, and I joined the Army at 18. I've always been interested in nature, science and biology. As a kid, I enjoyed finding frogs, lizards and other critters outside, but birds always struck me as somehow grander.

My interest in nature didn't change when I put on a uniform. Life in the Army involves quite a bit of outdoor time, so I have ample opportunity to explore and observe.

When you're in the military or in a warzone, everything is pretty bleak. I've always tried to find glimpses of beauty that slip through—a flower growing amid diesel generators, a sunset behind a guard tower or a magpie perched on a barbed wire.

Even though I'm not always in the most pleasant of situations, the birds have given me and others in my unit something to look forward to. While in Afghanistan, the Eurasian magpies fascinated me. I also liked seeing the different hawks and falcons, trying to compare them to the ones we have in the U.S.

Right now, the next chapter of my life will begin at Cambridge, Massachusetts, where the Army is sending me for graduate school at Harvard. I'm excited to see what birds I can find in the Boston area and what their migration patterns are. It'll be different than what I know along the Gulf Coast, where I've spent most of my life. But my interest in and love for birds, like all things in nature and the outdoors, will continue to grow in my journey through the Army and in life.

BRING BIRDING TO YOUR JOB

Here are some ideas for incorporating bird-watching into your daily routine.

DESK JOB. Use your breaks or lunch to take a walk or look for birds.
DRIVING JOB. Scan roadsides and telephone lines (safely) to see birds perched.
PEOPLE JOB. Whether you're a nurse or teacher, talk nature with others. It's something anyone can relate to.
OUTSIDE JOB. No excuses here—take time to notice the birds around you.
RETIRED. Let birds become part of your life. Volunteer with a local bird organization or nature center.

Bobbie holds a juvenile raptor (inset) that a sergeant rescued at his airfield in Afghanistan.

Wood duck
ducklings
*Photo by Steve and
Dave Maslowski*

Eastern bluebird
Photo by Bill Leaman

Black-capped chickadee
Grand Prize Winner in our
Backyard Photo Contest
Photo by James Ridley

Killdeer
Photo by rolfnussbaumer.com

Common yellowthroat
Finalist in our
Backyard Photo Contest
Photo by Ed Troche

amazing Hummingbirds

Discover activities every hummer lover should experience. Read about quick and easy ways to attract hummingbirds to your backyard. Learn expert tips for capturing these intriguing little fliers on camera.

TIM FITZHARRIS

A Bucket List for

Hummingbird Lovers

These activities, some silly and some seriously cool, are ones every hummingbird enthusiast should experience.

BY HEATHER LAMB

Several years ago

I was lucky enough to take a trip to southeastern Arizona where every destination, hike and tour focused on hummingbirds. My fellow travelers and I walked around starry-eyed, clutching cameras and scribbling field notes as we watched the tree branches and feeders. And we weren't disappointed; hummingbirds were everywhere. I spotted 13 different species on that trip, including several rarities.

The experience stuck with me, and made me realize that although watching hummingbirds at backyard sugar-water feeders is pretty wonderful, there are a lot of other ways to indulge that interest. This list of hummingbird activities is a good place to start. What are you waiting for?

Take a hummingbird vacation.

Southwestern states like Arizona, California, New Mexico and Texas offer the largest concentration of hummingbirds and a diverse range of hummingbird species. Destinations like Ramsey Canyon Preserve in Arizona or Davis Mountains State Park in Texas are especially known for plentiful and rare hummingbird sightings. But if such destinations are too far afield for you, take a day trip to a botanical garden that has plenty of sugar-water feeders. You'll see hummingbirds by the dozen, especially during fall migration.

Attend a hummingbird festival.

Hummingbird people are good people, and there's no better place to meet those kindred spirits than at a hummingbird festival. You can find these events all over the country. The festivals usually take place in July through September and are concentrated in areas that experience abundant migration activity. The Rockport-Fulton HummerBird Celebration in Texas and the Sedona Hummingbird Festival in Arizona are two of the best ones.

Start a hummingbird journal.

Here's an activity you can do without leaving home. Keep a journal of the hummingbird activity in your yard. Note when the first hummingbird arrives in spring and when the final one departs in fall. How many visit your feeders? How does their activity shift during the day? Notice changing factors like weather or feeder placement, and write down those funny hummingbird stories, too!

Get a hummingbird tattoo.

Real or temporary, a tattoo is a whimsical—or really devoted—way to acknowledge your love of hummingbirds. Smack that piece of dampened paper to your skin (or visit a reputable tattoo artist), and smile.

low-commitment temporary tattoo

Davis Mountains State Park in Texas is host to many species of hummingbirds.

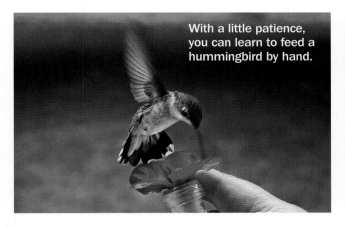

With a little patience, you can learn to feed a hummingbird by hand.

This hummingbird is being measured for banding.

Hand-feed a hummingbird.

Imagine the thrill of having a tiny hummingbird, which typically weighs 0.1 to 0.2 ounces (less than a marshmallow), alight on your palm. Give hand-feeding a whirl during nesting season or before migration, when the birds are expending a lot of energy and eating a lot of food. Spend time near your feeders, so the birds become accustomed to your presence. Then, cover all feeders but one, and hold that remaining feeder in your lap. Not every attempt will be successful, but be patient and keep trying.

Help band hummingbirds.

Researchers have been banding birds to gather information about migration, lifespan and population since 1920 as part of the North American Bird Banding Program. Hummingbird banding is an extremely specialized activity, with hummingbirds making up less than 1 percent of the birds banded. The banders themselves are an elite group, and hold special permits. Participate in the process by volunteering at banding events, which take place at hummingbird festivals, or during migration periods along key flyways.

Recognize hummingbird calls.

Experienced birders don't need binoculars to identify birds. They use their ears instead, and usually know a particular bird is nearby well before they spot it. Hummingbirds, though not known for their songs, still make a series of distinct calls. Become attuned to these sounds by finding recordings at websites like *allaboutbirds.org* to learn the calls of different hummingbirds and what they mean.

Share your hummingbird passion with others.

Thinking back to that Arizona hummingbird trip, one of its most enjoyable aspects was the shared experience. That sharing can happen on a trip, at a festival, on your front porch or at places like local schools and senior centers. Look for teaching or volunteering opportunities in your community to pass along what you love about hummingbirds. It's one experience that will surely make your life richer.

Find a nesting hummingbird.

Hummingbirds usually build their intricately engineered nests on tree branches, but sometimes the birds select more visible and unorthodox nesting spots like plant hooks, chandelier-style light fixtures or electrical wires. Any horizontal surface under a protective roof will usually do, though nests can be hard to find. Gather up your hummingbird-loving friends, and set out on the search.

Ruby-throated hummingbird, sitting on her nest

TOP 10
vines for hummingbirds

Attract hummers from the ground up with a few of their favorite blooming climbers.

BY MELINDA MYERS

TOP 10

If you want to grow vines, you might think you need a lot of space, but even if your planting area is limited, it's still possible to cultivate vines in containers on your patio, deck or balcony. But no matter where you decide to plant these vines—in containers or right in the garden—place them where you'll be able to enjoy the hummingbirds that will no doubt visit the nectar-filled blooms.

▲ Trumpet honeysuckle

LONICERA SEMPERVIRENS, ZONES 4 TO 9

Hummingbirds, butterflies and bees love native honeysuckle. Planting it in full sun or partial shade and moist soil will encourage the best flowering. The orange-red, trumpet-shaped flowers appear in clusters amongst the blue-green leaves, which persist through winter in southern states.

Why we love it: Unlike a lot of other plants, trumpet honeysuckle grows in clay soil and near black walnut trees.

▲ Mandevilla

MANDEVILLA, ANNUAL, PERENNIAL IN ZONES 10 TO 11

A drought-tolerant vine that can be grown in a container, hanging basket or right in the garden, mandevilla thrives in full sun to part shade and well-drained soil. You'll find many new cultivars with white, pink, maroon, crimson and bicolor flowers.

Why we love it: You can overwinter mandevilla indoors in a warm, sunny location.

◀ Cup and saucer vine

COBAEA SCANDENS, ANNUAL, PERENNIAL IN ZONES 9 TO 11

A vigorous grower, give this vine a sturdy support to climb and display its cup-shaped, aromatic flowers. The blooms open green and then mature to purple, lasting about four days. Grow in full sun and provide a bit of afternoon shade in hotter regions.

Why we love it: The flowers have a sweet musky fragrance and are reportedly pollinated by bats.

4

▲ Canary creeper

TROPAEOLUM PEREGRINUM, ANNUAL, PERENNIAL IN ZONES 9 TO 10

Take a close look at the bright yellow flowers and you'll see the inspiration for the common name. Grow this climbing nasturtium in full sun to part shade with moist, well-drained soil. Allow it to scramble through other plants, train it on a trellis or grow it in a hanging basket.

Why we love it: The sunny yellow flowers are showy and fragrant.

6

▲ Candy corn plant

MANETTIA LUTEORUBRA, ANNUAL, PERENNIAL IN ZONES 10 TO 11

This noncaloric candy corn is fun for gardeners of all ages. The orange tubular flowers are tipped in yellow, making them look like the Halloween treat. Grow it in full sun to light shade and moist, well-drained soil.

Why we love it: When the outdoor weather is too harsh, the candy corn plant can be grown indoors as a houseplant.

5

▲ Scarlet runner bean

PHASEOLUS COCCINEUS, ANNUAL

Grow scarlet runner bean, a hummingbird favorite, in a sunny spot in your vegetable or flower garden. You can grow these long vines on a trellis, arbor or fence. Regular harvesting will keep the plant producing more pods and keep its scarlet flowers blossoming.

Why we love it: The red blooms will brighten the landscape and lure hummingbirds. Plus, the edible beans will amp up your veggie options.

7

▲ Figwort

ASARINA SCANDENS, ANNUAL, PERENNIAL IN ZONES 9 TO 10

Brighten the summer and fall garden with the indigo, violet, pink or white flowers of figwort. Grow it in full sun to part shade on a trellis or allow the stems to spill over the edge of a hanging basket.

Why we love it: The flowers of this plant resemble snapdragons, which is why figwort is occasionally called climbing snapdragon.

8

▲ Purple passionflower

PASSIFLORA INCARNATA, ZONES 5 TO 9

Its unique flowers make this vine a standout in a sunny spot in the garden or in a container. You can even overwinter it as a houseplant. Also called maypop, this quick-spreading plant may need taming. Avoid using it with other species invasive to your area or you'll be overrun.
Why we love it: It's native to the southeast U.S. and also attracts butterflies.

9

▲ Trumpet vine

CAMPSIS RADICANS, ZONES 4 TO 9

This is the classic, well-known hummingbird vine. Native to the eastern U.S. and Canada, trumpet vine thrives in full sun and poor soils. Avoid excess fertilizer because it can retard flowering. Plant it in confined areas or mow suckers to keep it in check. It's important to note that it can be weedy or invasive in some southeastern states.
Why we love it: The orange-red trumpet flowers are a hummingbird favorite.

3 tips for selecting proper vine supports

Always choose structures that can handle the vine's weight and means of attachment.

- Twining and weaving vines need supports with wire frames or narrow legs and crossbars.
- Clinging vines require rough surfaces for rootlets and holdfasts to attach and support them.
- Many vines call for a guiding hand. Weave stems through and around the support and, if needed, attach plants with twine or soft twist ties.

10

▲ Hyacinth bean vine

DOLICHOS LABLAB, ANNUAL, PERENNIAL ZONES 10 TO 11

This purple beauty will quickly cover a trellis or fence and its green leaves, white, pink or purple-pink flowers and purple pods provide season-long color. Grow hyacinth bean in full sun to partial shade. Despite being an annual, it will often reseed in the garden.
Why we love it: The fragrant blooms are a treat for the senses. Plus, once it's established, this plant is drought-tolerant.

More plants for hummers

In addition to vines, you may also want to try some of these plants to attract more flying jewels to your backyard.

- **Firebush**
- **Monkey flower**
- **Penstemon**
- **Snowberry**
- **Autumn sage**
- **Milkweed**
- **Cardinal flower**
- **Bee balm**

- **Fuchsia**
- **Columbine**
- **Red hot poker**
- **Salvia**
- **Flowering tobacco**
- **Catmint**
- **Coral bells**

Bee balm

Hummingbird Sounds

Take note of the music of these little fliers, from hums to full song.

BY KENN AND KIMBERLY KAUFMAN

The male Anna's hummingbird is a champion singer.

Question: Why does a hummingbird hum? Answer: Because it can't remember the words!

OK, that's a pretty bad joke, but it addresses an interesting point. The humming for which hummingbirds are named isn't a vocal sound, but one created by the rapid beating of their wings. This isn't the only sound hummingbirds make. Let's take a look at other sounds you might hear.

Regular Calls

All hummingbirds make short, soft call notes. These are often useful for identifying species. In the West, for example, the soft *teew* of a black-chinned hummingbird is very different from the musical *chip* of a rufous hummingbird or the thin *tic* of a Costa's hummingbird.

Aggressive Calls

Hummingbirds are amazingly feisty creatures, constantly sparring over choice flower patches and feeders. Their aerial battles are mostly just bluffing, but they pump up the effect with all kinds of chattering, squealing noises. When a large number of hummingbirds gather, most of the sounds that you hear will be these aggressive calls.

Songs

Yes, some hummingbirds do sing! The champion singer among North American hummers is the male Anna's hummingbird, which is very common along the Pacific Coast. He will sit on a high perch and sing for minutes at a time, a scratchy series of notes punctuated by a loud *tzzip, tzzip*! The one at left is singing, but as you can see, it doesn't open its mouth very wide. In the desert Southwest, the male Costa's hummingbird also sings, but with a thin, piercing whistle, instead.

Costa's hummingbird

Although many kinds of tropical hummingbirds have noteworthy songs, most of those in North America aren't as accomplished as the Anna's or Costa's hummers. For example, what passes for song from the male ruby-throated hummingbird is just a monotonous series of calls, given mostly at dawn.

Wing and Tail Sounds

Many hummingbird sounds are produced by the feathers of the wings or tail vibrating against the air. The male broad-tailed hummingbird of the Rocky Mountain region has an especially impressive sound. You can always tell when an adult male broad-tail flies past, because of the high, metallic trilling of his wings.

Although the male ruby-throat's wing sounds are not as obvious, the pointed outer feathers of his wings create a high-pitched whine during his flight displays, while shorter inner feathers make a rattling sound when he changes directions.

The male Anna's hummingbird is famous for his song, but he also produces a remarkable sound with his tail feathers. His courtship display includes a zooming dive, in which he plummets toward the ground and then pulls up with a loud, explosive pop that can be heard from hundreds of yards away. Scientists used to debate whether this was a vocal sound, but studies have shown that it's the outer tail feathers vibrating at the bottom of the dive making the noise.

Listen carefully the next time you see a hummingbird. Not only will you hear that familiar hum of the wings, but you might be lucky enough to catch these other fun sounds.

hummer happenings

Your bird tales celebrate all things hummingbird.

hummingbird pit stop

When our crabapple tree is in full bloom, we watch the birds that use it as a resting spot between visits to our various bird feeders. We've spotted rose-breasted grosbeaks, orioles, cardinals, indigo buntings, finches and other birds in that crabapple tree. This photo is of a ruby-throated hummingbird, perched in the midst of the blossoms.

Rebecca Martin
STEVENS POINT, WISCONSIN

Fast Friends

While visiting from Florida, my granddaughter, Mira, made friends with a young hummingbird. I was amazed at how quickly she was able to entice this little bird, and she was absolutely thrilled when it perched on her finger. Mira named it Boomerang, because it kept coming back and seemed to be looking for her.

Sharon Deabler O'FALLON, MISSOURI

take your bath

While I was watering the flowers, I noticed the hummingbirds were sitting on the wet leaves and splashing around. I loved watching them so much, I set the hose up to keep spraying the leaves. Then I went to get the camera to start taking pictures. This was a young ruby-throated hummingbird bathing on the gerbera daisy leaves.

Mary Ann Bowyer
VESUVIUS, VIRGINIA

Nifty Nectar Trick

I've sometimes seen an Anna's hummingbird after the first snow, but it would leave after filling up on nectar or after my feeder froze. Then I tried a new approach: two feeders. When we had freezing weather and then snow, I defrosted one while the other was out, so that my Anna's always had food. This male quickly figured out my routine and seemed to pose for me while I replaced his favorite feeder.

Lynnette Mammino GRASS VALLEY, CALIFORNIA

Hungry Hummingbirds

While visiting my mother in Campbell, California, I went out on the deck of her 11th-floor apartment and was soon dive-bombed by a female Anna's hummingbird! My mother had taken down her feeder because of high winds, but I quickly hung it back up. The frisky flyer left, then came right back with eight friends! They allowed me to get very close for pictures.

It was a wonder to see six feeding at once. Back home, our ruby-throated hummingbirds are aggressive, so you don't often see more than one or two feeding at the same time, and they show up only after mid-March. What a treat the Anna's hummers were!

Pat Hyink ASHFORD, ALABAMA

THE
perfect SHOT

Fast and flighty hummingbirds can be tricky to spot, let alone capture in a faultless photo. We invited some of our favorite photographers to share their incredible photographs and their best advice for budding and veteran shutterbugs alike.

BY KAITLIN STAINBROOK

Give Yourself Options

Set your camera to its fastest motor drive speed and focus manually. Then, shoot hundreds of photos and pick the best ones in postproduction. There's no need for complicated flash setups. For natural results, shoot on overcast days and set your ISO speed to 1000 to 2000, which allows the wings to blur like it did here with this male rufous and female black-chinned. —*Tim Fitzharris*

▲ Create Perches

Collect dead branches and twigs, and incorporate them into your gardens and containers. The hummingbirds will use them when they're near their favorite food source, and supply you with an abundance of perched and posed opportunities. I took these three photos of ruby-throats (above, right and below) right in my own backyard.
—*Bud Hensley*

▶ Have Patience

Give hummingbirds time to get used to your presence before you start snapping away. This process may take a few days or even weeks. Watch your hummingbird visitors and wait for the right picture-taking opportunity. This could mean when they're perched like this juvenile hummingbird (right). Also, watch them feed. They tend to sip, back off from the feeder or flower, hover briefly, then sip again. Take advantage of their momentary feeding breaks to capture a photo.
—*Andrew Todzia*

▲ Get the Right Gear

Hummingbirds are creatures of habit. Train your camera on a bird's preferred perch, prefocus and shoot when it returns. A telephoto lens in the 300 mm to 500 mm range will work perfectly, especially one that can focus as close as 10 feet. Shutter speeds under 1/500th of a second or less will blur the bird's wings and shutter speeds of 1/2500th will freeze them. Wait for the bird to turn its head so you can catch the flashy iridescence in the throat patch, like with this calliope (above).

—*Ed Post*

▲ Look for Photo Ops

When it comes to taking pictures of hummingbirds, I've found the more natural the setting, the better. Like in this photo of an Anna's (above), which I took in my sister's backyard on the Fourth of July. Her landscaping is designed to attract hummingbirds, and they were really enjoying her Little Redhead crocosmia that day. I try to take advantage of flowers that hummingbirds are attracted to, like bee balm and foxglove. Remember, a great photo opportunity can come from anywhere, so keep your eyes peeled and your camera ready!

—*Daniel Ferneding*

▼ Keep Exploring

One of my favorite techniques for photographing hummingbirds is to catch them in flight, while they're coming to feeders or flowers. Setting up an outdoor studio with several flashes can lead to some truly spectacular results. It took several hours of perseverance in challenging lighting conditions to get this shot of a red-tailed comet (below) in the Andes Mountains of central Bolivia, but it was well worth the effort! With more than 300 species of hummingbirds in the world, there is no shortage of incredible species to photograph.

—*Glenn Bartley*

▲ Know Your Lighting

I'm always looking for a connection between birds and the plants they visit, because it tells the story of pollination, like this male green-crowned brilliant hummingbird posing on an ornamental banana flower (above). When it's rainy like this, I use fill flash to deal with the low light. In general, it's good to have technical knowledge of your camera and flash. This will allow you to capture good photos of these little flying jewels.

—*Gregory Basco*

Ruby-throated hummingbird in flowering dogwood

DID YOU KNOW? The yellow color on this hummingbird's throat is caused by a dusting of pollen.

Discourage Ants and Bees

Readers share tips for keeping pests away from hummingbird feeders.

1

Insert a Q-tip in one of the drinking ports, letting the tip stick out. The nectar travels up the stem to the cotton and the wasps and bees will sit on the tip and not bother the other feeding ports.

Dell Kyle
FAYETTEVILLE, GEORGIA

2

Bee guards work great for me. They are like little cages that fit into the feeder holes. The hummingbird's bill slides in and out easily, but it keeps the bees from reaching the sugar water.

Rebecca Williamson
BUSHNELL, ILLINOIS

3

To prevent ants from taking over your feeders, rub a very small coat of Vicks VapoRub on whatever your feeder hangs from. I've found that it doesn't bother the birds and the ants won't go near it.

Ruth Andren
GREENE, MAINE

4

Protect your feeder from ants by stringing it up with 8-lb. fishing line. The line is too narrow for the ants to traverse. I've used this trick successfully for many years.

Elizabeth Hodges
CLEMSON, SOUTH CAROLINA

5

Poke a hole in the middle of an old spray can cap. Run a wire to hang the feeder through the hole and put a dab of waterproof glue around the wire to prevent the ants from sneaking through. Then fill the cap with water.

Lisa Barlet
NEWBURG, NORTH DAKOTA

Sugar Water 101

*Make this the year you attract hummingbirds
(or increase their traffic) in your yard.*

The Recipe

If you haven't memorized the recipe yet, then now is the time. Combine four parts hot water to one part sugar. Mix it up until it's completely dissolved. Once it cools to room temperature, it's ready.

To Boil or Not to Boil

Using really hot water will usually suffice. However, if you plan on making extra sugar water to store in the fridge or you have so-so water quality, then it's best to boil.

Honey Do or Honey Don't?

Some people like to come up with creative ways to sweeten their sugar water without sugar, and the most common stand-in is honey. Not only is honey a bad idea in general, but it can also make your sugar-water mixture ferment more quickly. Skip the honey, and stick to sugar.

The Red Dye Debate

Even though every bird authority around the country seems to agree that you don't need red dye, people still add it to their sugar water. You also see companies offering premade sugar water that is red. If this is you, don't feel bad—but it's time to break this habit once and for all. You don't need red water to attract hummingbirds. In fact, it could be bad for the birds (scientists are still figuring this one out). Either way, it's not worth the risk.

The Important Extras

Sugar water eventually goes bad, unless you're lucky enough to have a busy feeder that the hummingbirds quickly empty. You should be in the habit of changing it every few days or even sooner if it's really hot out. Also, don't forget to clean your feeders occasionally. Mold can collect, so you want to make sure you're offering hummingbirds clean, safe water.

> **BACKYARD TIP**
> Add another sugar-water feeder in late summer when migration increases. This will help keep feisty males from fighting for space.

reader advice

Need clever tips for cleaning the nooks and crannies of your sugar-water feeders? Our readers can help.

I rinse my feeders with vinegar, and they stay clean. I rinse them every time I change the food. It's so easy and works well.
Mattie Stillwell
TENAHA, TEXAS

I keep a box of parakeet gravel on hand to clean my feeders. Put a couple of teaspoons in the feeder with warm water, then swirl and rise. It cleans the toughest mold.
Sally Brovold
KULM, NORTH DAKOTA

I don't mind cleaning my hummingbird feeders except for all those little yellow bee guards. I found an easy way to do it, though. Take any juice bottle that has a wide opening and add 3 cups of water along with $\frac{1}{8}$ cup of bleach. Add the bee guards, replace the cap and shake. Then let it sit for five minutes and shake again. Once you take them out and rinse them well, you'll have clean bee guards.

Marija Domijan
ST. LOUIS, MISSOURI

Rufous hummingbird

Make a DIY hummingbird feeder.

Creating your own sugar-water feeder is simple, and if you're crafty, you've probably already built one or maybe a dozen. For the rest of us, Pinterest (or *birdsandblooms.com*) offers ideas. Make an easy DIY sugar-water feeder with a pretty glass bottle, some copper wire, a stopper and a tube. Look for wire in several gauges at craft stores. Find the stopper and tube attachments online by searching "hummingbird feeder tube."

glad you asked!

Kenn and Kimberly Kaufman answer your hummingbird questions.

Rufous hummingbird on Rocky Mountain bee plant

BACKYARD TIP
Female and young male ruby-throats look similar, so you might have more visitors than you think.

◄ I use about a gallon of sugar water a day. Is it possible to determine how many hummingbirds I feed by the amount of sugar water they drink in a day?
Marge Kaufman SIGEL, ILLINOIS

Kenn and Kimberly: According to lab studies, the amount of sugar water consumed by a hummingbird will vary depending on the richness of the sugar concentration. With the typical 4:1 ratio of water to sugar, a ruby-throat probably won't drink more than about 2 fluid ounces per day. A gallon of sugar water could feed about 60 hummingbirds in a day! The number of individuals could be even higher if some are just stopping briefly, or it could be lower if some of the sugar water is being lost to evaporation, insects, etc. It's tricky to come up with solid numbers, but it's still fun to ponder how many might be out there.

▲ For two weeks last winter, a rufous hummingbird visited. Is this unusual for north-central Florida in January? We usually have ruby-throats.
Walton Robey OCALA, FLORIDA

Kenn and Kimberly: Years ago, we would have said it was very unusual. At one time, almost all rufous hummingbirds spent the winter in southern Mexico. But these little pioneers have been expanding their winter range into the Southeastern U.S. for the last few decades, and hundreds now stay through the season along the Gulf Coast from Texas to Florida, and north as far as the Carolinas. The ruby-throat is still the expected hummingbird in Florida for most of the year, but in midwinter you're just as likely to spot a rufous.

We're selling our house, and I'm concerned the new owners will not keep the hummingbird feeders filled. What will happen?

Vincent Staley FREDERICKSBURG, VIRGINIA

Kenn and Kimberly: We appreciate your concern, but hummingbirds are adaptable and good at finding new places to live. In natural habitats, good concentrations of flowers may change over time. For example, a meadow filled with flowers one year may be overgrown with shrubs the next. Hummingbirds have to be able to move around and find new food sources. Of course, if you can talk to the new residents of your home, you could try to inspire them with stories about the magic of hummingbirds and tell them the rewards of keeping the feeders filled and clean.

▼ On an early summer evening, I was sitting on the patio and saw a female ruby-throated hummingbird at some coral bells. A male appeared and they flew together, spiraling into the air about 75 feet! Is this a mating ritual?

Jenifer Junkins TORONTO, IOWA

Kenn and Kimberly: We wish we could say that the male was just being romantic, but it's more likely that he was trying to chase her away. Male ruby-throats are combative little guys, and when they've found a good patch of flowers, they usually respond to others of their kind by trying to chase them away. If the other hummer is a male, they may have a brief fight before one of them leaves. If the intruder is a female, the male may start by chasing and then gradually shift over to something that looks more like courtship displays.

▶ I never get more than one hummingbird at a time at my feeders. How can I encourage them to share?

Cheryl Vandermark WALLKILL, NEW YORK

Kenn and Kimberly: Hummingbirds have an instinct to protect their food sources, because in nature, a patch of flowers will produce only so much nectar in a day. The tiny birds carry this defensiveness over to artificial feeders. The best way to keep one hummingbird from dominating a feeder is to put up several feeders in different spots. If some feeders can be out of sight from the others (around a corner, for example), it will be even harder for one bird to control them all. With multiple feeders available, even the more aggressive hummers may give up and just share with others.

BACKYARD TIP
If you have an aggressive hummingbird chasing other birds away, set up a second feeder far from the first one.

 **FAQ** "We were finally successful in attracting ruby-throated hummingbirds with feeders. Now that we've attracted them, will the same group and their offspring return to our backyard next year?"

Dennis Woods GREENSVILLE, ONTARIO

Kenn and Kimberly: Now that you've had success in attracting the ruby-throats, there's a good chance they'll come back every year. Young hummingbirds usually return to the general area where they were hatched. In addition, hummingbirds have strong spatial memory, and they may return to the same spots where they've found food in the past, even after migrating thousands of miles. If you have feeders and flowers ready at the right season, you can expect to have plenty of hummingbirds.

amazing hummingbirds

Ruby-throated hummingbird
Photo by rolfnussbaumer.com

Male Anna's hummingbird
Photo by Lynne McClure

Ruby-throated hummingbird
Photo by Dennis J. McNeill

Anna's hummingbird
Finalist in our
Backyard Photo Contest
Photo by Joey Paynter

Female ruby-throated hummingbird
Photo by Janice Neitzel

CHAPTER 3

DIY Backyard

Create a beautiful and bird-friendly backyard with easy do-it-yourself projects. Find creative ways to reuse everyday items in the garden. Get inspired by these clever creations.

JIM WEILAND/RDAEB

growing
outside

When it comes to gardening in small spaces, your options aren't limited to a square wooden box. There are plenty of ways to make a fabulous, one-of-a-kind garden bed or container with a little work and some imagination.

While there are no rules in raised beds or containers, there are a few things to keep in mind: proper drainage, adequate protection from critters and gardener accessibility. And never plant edibles in treated wood. Most important, have fun and embrace your creativity.

the box

Add charm to your garden with these container and raised bed ideas that are anything but ordinary. BY CRYSTAL RENNICKE

If that old boat or canoe springs a leak, fill it with flowers!

1. Long-Lost Hobby Equipment

When hobbies lose their luster, use the goods for the garden.

Drum Set. Turn your drum set dreams into garden glory. Remove the drumhead, plant the drum shell partway into the ground, then add soil and plants.

Boat or canoe. If your vessel has sprung a leak, reuse it for flowers. Someday you'll catch that 50-inch musky, but for now, flowers are much easier than fish.

Instruments. Trumpets, guitars and banjos all have potential to hold flowers. Plus, they're almost guaranteed to be good conversation pieces.

Leftover paint. Aspiring artists typically have paint to spare. Use your skills to fancy up your existing raised beds. It doesn't have to be perfect; in fact, just a solid bright color will perk up your plantings.

2. Forlorn Furniture

Updating furniture in your home? Give your old stuff an extended life outside.

Bed frame. When painted a bright color, an old wooden bed frame looks fabulous propped outdoors and planted with lovely flowers, creating a literal raised bed.

Bookcase. A saggy-shelf bookcase easily transforms into a raised bed by removing the back (and shelves, if you wish), laying it on its side and filling it with soil, flowers or veggies. Worms and bookworms alike will love it.

Drawers. Turn dinged-up dresser drawers into small raised plots for herbs or other special plants by adding wooden boards for legs and a coat or two of paint.

File cabinets. Paint old file cabinet drawers a vibrant color to make small beds for flowers. It's more fun than using them for old tax documents or bank statements.

3. Empty Nester Supplies

When kids grow out of their childhood things, repurpose them into items for growing plants.

Outgrown goods. If they outgrow their boots, plant flowers in them. Turn a used crib into a garden bed. Old changing table? An instant display for containers!

Kiddie pools. Those plastic pools are only useful when the kids are pint-size. Add drainage holes and you've got yourself a handy and portable raised bed.

Swing set. Many parts of a wooden swing set can be reused in the garden. If a sandbox was attached, make it into a raised planter. The ropes and chains can support climbing plants. A tire swing can become a hanging flower bed.

4. Just Plain Quirky

Looking for something fun and unique? These ideas take your garden from ordinary to off-the-wall.

Interlocking blocks. The little kid inside you will love this Lego-like raised bed growing set. After a successful Kickstarter campaign, Togetherfarms sells these awesome raised bed kits on Amazon for around $70. They are made from food-safe recycled plastic and are easily assembled like Legos—no tools necessary.

Watering troughs. Though normally meant for farm duty, these galvanized multipurpose bins look sleek planted with bright flowers or vegetables. You can find them at farm merchandise stores or by asking a generous farmer who's getting rid of one.

Raised Bed Freebies

Get materials for your raised beds for free! Here are some ideas to help you save.

- Check websites such as freecycle.org and craigslist.org often. These are great sources for free or cheap items around your area.
- Scour the imperfect bin at your local lumber or hardware store for wood at a reduced rate. Since it's going outside to be filled with soil, it doesn't need to be perfect.
- Check out local flea markets, garage sales or estate sales for big bargains.

Plain Pot Makeover

Give boring plastic pots a fresh, new look. With a little glue and scrap fabric, you can have designer-grade pots without spending a dime.

Wrap It Use burlap or an old tablecloth, and cut it to wrap snugly around the pot. Then, hot-glue or use decoupage glue to secure. Or try using cording tightly wound around the entire pot.

If you're displaying the pots outside, spray them with a coat of outdoor sealant.

A Bird for the Birds

This little birdhouse is simple, sweet and versatile. If you can find a box that matches the approximate size needed, then you'll be able to make this birdhouse almost before you can say "black-capped chickadee!"

BY ALISON AUTH

Step 11

Step 12

supplies

- **5-in. square box (built, reclaimed or purchased)**
- **Lauan for "bird" shape**
- **Small finish nails**
- **Picture-hanging hardware or wire and 2 screws**
- **1-in. butt hinge**
- **Screen door hook and eye**
- **Glue**
- **Exterior latex primer and paint**
- **Shellac or other outdoor varnish**
- **Bird template**
- **Jigsaw**
- **Screw gun or drill**
- **1¼-in. to 1½-in. hole saw**
- **Clamps**
- **Hammer**
- **Fine-grit sandpaper**

come together to form a perfect square. Clamp until dry.

STEP 4. Once dry, reinforce the joints with small finish nails or brads.

STEP 5. Sand box with fine-grit sandpaper in preparation for painting.

CUT OUT BIRD SHAPE

STEP 6. Use a photocopier to enlarge the red bird pattern (below) 200%. Or print out the template (at *birdsandblooms.com/birdpattern*) and cut out the bird shape.

STEP 7. Trace bird onto lauan; cut out with the jigsaw.

STEP 8. Using a hole saw attached to a screw gun or drill, bore a 1¼-in. to 1½-in. hole in the lauan. This is the bird's entrance, so be sure to place it accordingly.

STEP 9. Sand the face and edges smooth in preparation for painting.

PAINT AND ASSEMBLE

STEP 10. Prime and paint the outside of the box and bird shape, leaving the inside unpainted.

BIRD PATTERN

Use a photocopier to enlarge pattern 200%.

STEP 11. Hinge the bird cutout to the box using a simple 1-in. butt hinge or similar connector (see photo above).

STEP 12. Attach screw-eye with hook to the back of the bird and the other screw-eye to the side of the box so that they meet when the hook closes (see photo above).

STEP 13. Seal the outside of birdhouse with several coats of shellac.

STEP 14. Attach picture-hanging hardware to the back of the box.

NOTE If you are building the box, follow the instructions from step 1. If you already have a box, begin with step 6.

STEP 1. Cut one 5x5-in. square, two 5x4¾-in. rectangles and two 4¾x4½-in. rectangles out of ¼-in. plywood, clear pine, shelf board, barn board or similar.

STEP 2. Glue one 5x4¾-in. rectangle to one 4¾x4½-in. rectangle. The 4¾-in. dimension is the height of both rectangles. Once joined, they will form an "L" with a short side, and a longer side but both the same height. Clamp until dry. Repeat with the other 2 rectangles.

STEP 3. Glue the two L-shaped side sections to the 5-in. square box bottom. Make sure that the sections

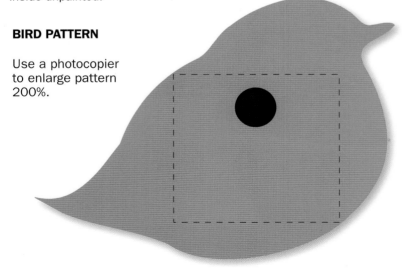

DIY TIP We like the burlap of this background, but you could also do a solid color or design.

Moss Letter Art

This easy art project is inspired by nature.

BY VANESSA TSUMURA

supplies

- 8-in. papier-mache letter
- 8x10-in. frame
- 14x12-in. piece of burlap
- 18x16-in. piece of SuperMoss Instant Green Moss Mat
- Marker
- Glue gun
- Brads

STEP 1. Place letter on the back of the moss mat and trace the shape with a marker. Cut out and hot-glue to the front of the letter.

STEP 2. Measure the thickness of the letter and cut strips of equal width from moss. Hot-glue the strips to the sides of the letter.

STEP 3. Remove glass from frame.

STEP 4. Cover the backing board with burlap and trim to size. Glue to board at corners.

STEP 5. Apply hot glue to the back of the letter and place the letter in the center of the burlap-covered board.

STEP 6. When dry, flip the board over and hammer brads into the back of the letter about 4 in. apart.

STEP 7. Place the backing in the frame and secure in place.

Divine Wagon Divan

Transform the classic little red wagon into a charming seat.
Whether you're doing fall yard cleanup or spring planting,
this wagon lounge goes where you go.

BY ALISON AUTH

supplies

- Radio Flyer Classic Red Wagon with rim (any model)
- 4x8-ft. sheet of ⅝-in. thick exterior-grade plywood
- 1x2-in. piece of wood for wagon perimeter
- 2x6-in. board cut to desired width of the bench seat and back
- 3-in. square posts
- Construction adhesive
- Wood screws
- Exterior latex semi-gloss primer and paint
- Jigsaw
- Screw gun

STEP 1. Create the bench seat by flipping the wagon upside down and tracing its outline in pencil onto the plywood. Add 2 ⅝-in. to all sides; cut out with a jigsaw.

STEP 2. Cut another piece from the plywood that is slightly smaller than the interior dimensions of the wagon for a stabilizer panel. Screw the stabilizer panel to the center of the bench seat. Position bench seat on the wagon with the stabilizer panel inside.

STEP 3. Cut a 1x2-in. board long enough to surround the wagon's perimeter. Depending on the size of your wagon, you may need to use more than one board.

STEP 4. Screw the board to the underside of the bench where it hangs over the wagon rim. There should be a ⅝-in. space around the perimeter of the plywood. By sandwiching the wagon rim between the bench seat and board, the entire bench assemblage will be secured to the wagon.

Make decorative flowers to dress up your seat!

(Tip: This is easiest to do with the wagon assemblage upside down.)

STEP 5. Draw bench back onto the plywood and cut out with a jigsaw. The bench back should be the same width as the bench seat.

STEP 6. Cut a 2x6-in. board the width of the bench seat. Apply construction adhesive to the bottom of the board and attach to the back of the bench seat. Screw in place from the bottom of the bench seat and the bench back to secure.

STEP 7. Cut armrests out of 3-in. posts. Apply construction adhesive and screw in place from the bottom of the bench seat, making sure the armrests are flush with the front of the bench seat and fit snugly against the bench back.

STEP 8. Measure and draw the decorative apron for the bench seat out of remaining plywood. Screw the decorative apron to the 1x2-in. board from Step 3. The apron should be flush with the front edge of the bench seat.

STEP 9. Prime and paint, then add your favorite cushions and pillows!

HEIDI HESS

Chandelier Birdhouse and Planter

With just a few tweaks to a rummage sale find, you can create this elegant planter that also doubles as a birdhouse.

BY THE EDITORS OF *BIRDS & BLOOMS*

supplies

- **5-light chandelier with chain (search yard sales, thrift stores and Craigslist for bargains)**
- **Four 4½-in. terra-cotta pots**
- **Unfinished wood birdhouse, approximately 9x4x4-in.**
- **Epoxy putty**
- **Outdoor primer and spray paint**
- **Large S-hook**
- **1¼-in. hardwood dowel or rod**
- **Newspaper**
- **2 sawhorses**

STEP 1. Twist off bulbs, candle tubes and sockets. Discard.

STEP 2. Disassemble chandelier and remove all wires.

STEP 3. Fill all openings in chandelier with epoxy putty. Follow manufacturer's instructions.

STEP 4. Attach the birdhouse to a bobeche using putty.

STEP 5. Knead putty into four pea-sized balls and place along the bottom edges of a pot.

STEP 6. Attach to the center of a bobeche.

STEP 7. Repeat with the remaining pots and dry according to product directions.

STEP 8. Hang the chandelier from the dowel and prop up with sawhorses.

STEP 9. Apply a coat of primer to the chandelier. Follow manufacturer's instructions.

STEP 10. Apply at least two coats of spray paint to the chandelier. Follow manufacturer's instructions.

STEP 11. When dry, drape the chain over a tree branch and attach it to the chandelier with an S-hook.

diy backyard   93

Bowling Pin Butterfly

An old bowling pin can metamorphose into a beautiful butterfly with this striking pair of wings made from plywood. Try painting different wing patterns and let your imagination soar!

BY ALISON AUTH

supplies

- Printer (optional)
- Pre-primed lauan plywood
- Four L-brackets and screws
- Medium or fine grit sandpaper
- Bowling pin
- Stiff wire or coat hanger for antennae
- Galvanized wire for hanging
- Primer
- Spray paint
- Acrylic craft paints
- Exterior-grade spray varnish
- Paintbrush
- Super glue
- Needle-nose pliers
- Craft knife
- Drill and small bit
- Jigsaw

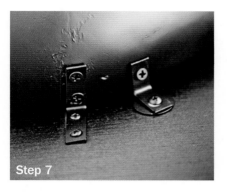

Step 7

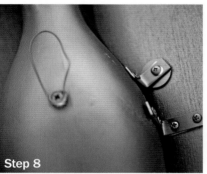

Step 8

STEP 1. Enlarge to desired size and tile-print the free downloadable butterfly wing stencil available at *birdsandblooms.com/bowlingbutterfly*. Or draw the butterfly wing freehand.

STEP 2. Cut out the wing stencil and, if desired, the inner detailing. Trace outline and detailing onto the plywood with a pencil, then flip the stencil and repeat to create wings that are mirror images of each other.

STEP 3. Using a jigsaw, cut out the butterfly wings. Lightly sand the wings until smooth.

STEP 4. Prep bowling pin by drilling two holes for antennae in the top using a drill bit slightly larger than the diameter of the wire.

STEP 5. Prime the bowling pin or use a spray paint with primer. Spray paint the bowling pin and allow to dry.

STEP 6. Paint wing design using acrylic paint. Let dry.

STEP 7. Drill holes on side of bowling pin to affix wings. Attach wings using two L-brackets per wing and screws.

STEP 8. Center a screw to the back of the bowling pin for hanging. Using needle-nose pliers, wrap galvanized wire around the head of the screw to form a loop.

STEP 9. Cut wire antennae to desired length, then use pliers to twist ends, forming a small decorative loop on each. Drop small amounts of super glue into antenna holes, then insert antennae. Keep butterfly upright until glue dries.

STEP 10. Spray butterfly with several coats of exterior-grade spray varnish. Once dry, hang and properly secure butterfly to a gardening shed or tree.

HEIDI HESS

Miniature Pond

Create a calming oasis on your patio with an easy, do-it-yourself pond. You don't even need fancy pumps—just water.

BY ALISON AUTH

supplies

- **Watertight container**
- **Water plants**
- **Garden soil (heavy clay)or aquatic plant soil**
- **Pea gravel (if using garden soil)**
- **Black plastic pots**
- **Mosquito Dunks**

the plants

Look for three types of aquatic plants for your water garden.

1. EMERGENTS. They are potted and have great foliate. Try umbrella palm and dwarf cattails.

2. SUBMERGED. They live below the surface of the water and add oxygen. Try anacharis.

3. FLOATERS. They float on the water's surface. Try water hyacinth and parrot's feathers.

STEP 1. Choose your pond container. Materials like ceramic, concrete, plastic, terra-cotta, metal or porcelain are great options. Don't use wood unless you line it with black plastic. Remember that the pot will get heavy, so place it where you want to display it before filling it with water.

STEP 2. Put plants in the black plastic pots. If you use heavy garden soil (high in clay content), you're all set. Just cover the soil with an inch or two of pea gravel to keep it from floating to the top of your pond. If using aquatic plant soil, bury a fertilizer tab with each plant.

STEP 3. Place potted plants at the appropriate depths in the empty pond container. I used pieces of brick to set my potted plants at the right level. You could also use upside-down terra-cotta or ceramic pots, pieces of stone, or plastic lunch containers filled with sand. Plant from deep to shallow, and from large to small.

STEP 4. Now add water. Start by adding water to the potted plants themselves. After the pond is full, add floater plants and a chunk of a Mosquito Dunks doughnut.

quick tip

If you have flowers growing in your garden, snip a couple of blooms and add them to your water garden just like you would a vase.

HEIDI HESS

welcome, Wildlife!

It's easy to create a backyard haven for birds and wildlife. Discover gardening secrets, innovative feeding ideas and other proven tips for attracting a flurry of activity.

CATHYKEIFER/ISTOCK.COM

grow a goldfinch garden

With the right flowers, your backyard can

be a goldfinch sanctuary. BY HEATHER LAMB

Male goldfinch on black-eyed Susan

There's nothing worse than a vacant goldfinch feeder. After all, they're supposed to be a sure thing, right? Last year, when my family and I moved from Wisconsin to Missouri, one of the first things to go up in the new backyard, right outside the kitchen window, was a tube feeder filled with nyjer. I wanted those American goldfinches where I could see them. But weeks went by and the feeder was quiet. The nyjer remained untouched.

I knew a big part of the reason was the new habitat. Among yards with more lawn grass than native flowers and shrubs, the area wasn't a natural fit for goldfinches, which prefer open, weedy fields with shrubby edges. It got me thinking: *What if I could lure goldfinches with plants that would make them give my yard a chance?*

The Goldfinch Appeal

These birds are like the gregarious neighbors at the block party, the ones everyone wants to talk to. The males' bright yellow summer plumage, their cheery call and willingness to approach bird feeders—except mine—make them popular backyard guests. And they're prevalent, too. Their range extends across the U.S. and southern Canada from east to west. In the 2014 Great Backyard Bird Count, the American goldfinch was the sixth-most reported bird.

The goldfinch diet consists almost entirely of seeds. So if you're growing with goldfinches in mind, seed-producing plants are essential. Their penchant for thistle seeds is well known (more on that later), and they'll seek out the seeds of plants in the massive *Asteraceae (Compositae)* family, including sunflower, black-eyed Susan, purple coneflower and aster. They also gravitate toward grasses and weedy plants. Some bird-watchers also swear that yellow flowers attract goldfinches. And while the ornithological jury is out on that assertion, adding goldenrod, yellow zinnias or blanket flowers to the mix can't hurt.

Green-headed (aka cutleaf) coneflower is a good wildflower to plant for seedeaters.

Photographer Marie Read says to go native with your plants. This is her yard, and it works for her.

Plants to grow for seeds: cup plant, goldenro

Sunflowers are one of the best options to attract goldfinches.

Joe Pye weed, purple coneflower and sunflower

Grow the Right Stuff

To identify a few other plant options, I talked with people who spend a lot of time watching birds—wildlife photographers. In her upstate New York yard, photographer Marie Read tends a native plant garden that's just for the birds. There she plants towering cutleaf coneflowers (*Rudbeckia laciniata*) for goldfinches, and also sees the birds on her Joe Pye weed and cup plant (*Silphium perfoliatum*).

And of course, there's that thistle. "Thistle is their No. 1 choice—that's guaranteed," says another photographer, Dave Maslowski. He and brother Steve have spent five decades shooting wildlife photos, mostly of birds. Not only are thistle seeds attractive to goldfinches, the birds famously use down from mature plants to line their nests. It's one reason the American goldfinch nests so late in the season, usually between late June and early August. The problem with thistle is that many types are invasive. When planting, look for natives like field thistle (*Cirsium discolor*), Flodman's thistle (*C. flodmanii*) and wavyleaf thistle (*C. undulatum*), while also checking to make sure the variety isn't a nuisance in your area. (The U.S. Department of Agriculture's invasive and noxious plant listing at *plants.usda.gov* is a good resource.)

Thistle isn't the only material female goldfinches use to line their nests. Milkweed, cattails and dandelion are other options, as are willow catkins and cottonwood fluff. But the birds will use whatever is available, says Robyn Bailey, project director of the Cornell Lab of Ornithology's NestWatch. (Learn how you can get involved in the project at *nestwatch.org*.) It's part of what makes the birds so fascinating: They are incredibly adaptable to their environment.

One plant to eliminate from a goldfinch habitat is burdock. While feeding on the seeds, goldfinches can become entangled in the multiple burrs of this plant and die.

Goldfinches at thistle feeders

Plant Nesting Sites

Given the goldfinch's habitat, it should come as no surprise that "shrubby" is a fair description of their nesting sites. Although goldfinches will nest in taller trees, more typical placement is in a shaded location on a low, dense shrub or tree 3 to 10 feet from the ground, Robyn says. And the birds aren't specialists. "They'll use whatever is dominant in their habitats," Robyn says. "In more swampy areas with tamarack, they'll use tamarack. In an old field with hawthorn, they'll use hawthorn."

More important are the characteristics of the shrubs and trees. "Their nest is very much a cup shape, so if they can get access to a more supported structure they'll use that," Robyn says. Goldfinches often build nests in a vertical fork, where three or more branches meet to form the perfect spot for that cup shape. Plants like dogwood, elderberry, buttonbush and hawthorn are common, as are Monterey pine, willow and fruit trees. They'll even nest in thistle plants that have the right structure, Robyn adds.

For cover before or after nesting season, goldfinches seek out many of those same types of plants, as well as low, dense evergreens, especially in winter.

As a wildlife photographer, Marie has an appreciation for birds that put on a bit of a show, and the American goldfinch fits that description. "They're very acrobatic," Marie says. "They won't just perch on a flower. Goldfinches cling. They will feed upside down."

With the proper plantings, I'm looking forward to seeing some acrobatic shows again in my own yard. In a fitting conclusion to my lonely-feeder saga, as I was working on this article, I looked out my kitchen window to see a group of goldfinches at the feeder. They were juveniles, or so I assumed from their dull coloring and slightly frenetic behavior. They fluttered around awkwardly, taking turns at the half-empty feeder. I smiled. Now the new place truly felt like home.

Goldfinch in crabapple

Goldfinch nest

Sunflowers for Birds

It's one of the best plants you can have in your garden—find out why.

Pick the Right Variety

You can find many sunflower options on the market today, but not all of them are suitable food sources for birds. When selecting sunflowers, make sure they produce a good supply of seeds. Some of our top picks include Mammoth Grey Stripe, Paul Bunyan and Aztec Gold.

Growing Tips

Sunflowers are truly one of the easiest plants to grow, but they do have a few requirements. They need at least six hours of sunlight per day and well-drained soil. They benefit from organic matter, and also keep the area under sunflowers mulched for better results.

Ready for Seeds

Sunflowers have the best seed buffet in late summer to early fall. For longer harvest time, stagger your planting, early spring to midsummer. This way, you can attract birds for months.

Harvest Tip

Gather your sunflower heads, and put them in a dry place to dehydrate. You can then hang them out by your feeders, extending the sunflower season all the way into fall.

American goldfinch

Black-capped chickadee

BRING IN THE BIRDS

Here are some species you may attract by planting sunflowers.

- Cardinals
- Chickadees
- House finches
- Titmice
- Grosbeaks
- Nuthatches
- Goldfinches
- Red-bellied woodpeckers
- Pine siskins

Black-capped chickadees are leaders of the winter flocks.

mixed winter flocks

Watch for the cold-season behavior of common bird species traveling together in large packs.

BY KENN AND KIMBERLY KAUFMAN

Dark-eyed junco

It's not uncommon for still, silent winter landscapes to be suddenly disrupted by distant birdcalls. Within moments, half a dozen kinds of birds appear, flitting among tree branches, climbing up trunks, hanging upside down from twigs. For just a few minutes, the birds bring life to the area with colors, sounds and movement. Then they all fly away together. These mixed flocks of birds are one of winter's special features. If you're aware of the activity, you may be able to observe them practically anywhere in North America, and possibly in your own backyard.

Safety in Numbers

So why do we see these mixed flocks? It's probably not just because birds enjoy one another's company. For many, there's a good reason for flocking: It's safer than traveling alone. Searching for food out in the wild takes lots of concentration, and it's hard to look for seeds or berries and watch for danger at the same time. With more birds in the flock, there's a better chance that a swooping hawk or prowling cat will be spotted while there's still time to sound the alarm and make a getaway.

Leaders of the Pack

When you see a mixed flock moving through the trees, it may seem as if they're all acting independently. But there are definite leaders and followers.

In treetop flocks, the leaders are usually chickadees. These busy, acrobatic little birds live in pairs or family groups during the summer, but in winter they gather in groups of a dozen or more. These flocks stick together throughout the cold months. As they make a regular circuit through the woods, other small birds fall in with

Northern cardinals, a tufted titmouse and a black-capped chickadee share a feeder.

them, following the lead of the chickadees—nuthatches, brown creepers, titmice, kinglets, downy woodpeckers and yellow-rumped warblers among them. These birds are clued in to the voices of their chickadee leaders, and when they hear an alarm note, they immediately look around for any sign of danger.

North America has several species of chickadees in different regions—including black-capped chickadees across the Northern states and Canada, Carolina chickadees in the Southeast, mountain chickadees in the Rocky Mountain region and chestnut-backed chickadees in the Pacific Northwest—but they all serve as flock leaders in their own areas.

These busy, acrobatic little birds live in pairs or family groups during the summer, but in winter they gather in groups of a dozen or more.

Black-capped chickadee

Woodpeckers, nuthatches and creepers examine the bark of trunks and large limbs, with the nuthatches often going down trees headfirst.

White-breasted nuthatch

Pine siskins and American goldfinches

Zone Defense

Active and alert, chickadees may be quicker to spot danger than the other birds that flock with them. For example, brown creepers, creeping up trees with their faces close to the bark, can't be scanning in all directions as easily as a chickadee can.

The followers may not help the chickadees much, but they don't do any harm, either. They usually aren't competing for the same food because they all seek nutrition in different ways. Woodpeckers, nuthatches and creepers examine the bark of trunks and large limbs, with the nuthatches often going down trees headfirst. Kinglets may hover under the tips of twigs, while titmice often hang upside down from heavier branches. So several kinds of birds can forage in the same tree without any direct competition.

It might seem as if the same birds are traveling with the chickadees all day, but that isn't necessarily so. Some of these birds have their own winter territories, and they'll stay with the flock only while it travels through their own corner of the woods. A white-breasted nuthatch, for instance, will follow right along with the chickadees until they come to the edge of its territory—then it will drop out, and another nuthatch from the neighboring territory will take its place in the flock.

Male and female northern cardinals

Flocks at the Feeder

These winter flocks like to keep moving. Instinct tells them to travel within their home range so that they don't use up all the food in any one spot. So even if you have a backyard filled with bountiful bird feeders, a flock is likely to arrive, stay for a short while and then move on. Don't worry, though: It will be back, perhaps several times a day.

Treetop flocks led by chickadees represent only one kind of mixed winter flock. There are also mixed flocks of seed-eating birds that live close to the ground, often including dark-eyed juncos, American tree sparrows, white-throated sparrows, white-crowned sparrows and others. Another type of winter flock may include goldfinches, pine siskins and redpolls.

Keep an eye out for these winter flocks, either out in the woods or among the birds that visit your yard. When you spot one of these mixed gatherings, watch to see how the different species interact, and see if you can figure out which birds are the leaders and which are the followers. You'll find that these diverse flocks add variety and excitement to your winter birding.

4 Ways to Attract Mixed Flocks This Winter

PROVIDE COVER. Birds seek protection from predators and from extreme weather. Pine, cedar and spruce are great options in all seasons, but especially in winter. Winter visitors will also appreciate brush piles you can make out of fallen limbs and branches.

SERVE GOOD EATS. Black-oil sunflower seed, peanuts and suet provide important nutrients in winter. For some birds in mixed flocks, berries are also important. Some of our backyard favorites are serviceberry, dogwood, juniper, wild grape and viburnum.

PUT OUT GROUND FEEDERS. Some winter flocks include juncos and native sparrows, which prefer to forage on or near the ground. A low tray-style feeder is best, but in a pinch you can sprinkle seed directly on the ground or on packed snow.

OFFER FRESH WATER. In areas with wintry weather, open water can be hard to find. Winter flocks are much more likely to visit a backyard birdbath with fresh water. Keep the water clean and consider adding a birdbath heater.

Weasel in winter

winter wildlife

Be on the lookout for these cold-weather guests this season.

BY DAVID MIZEJEWSKI

As winter deepens and cold winds blow, you might think all creatures have fled to warmer climes. In reality, there are plenty of wildlife visitors. Be on the lookout for these species and their signs this winter.

Flying Squirrels

Flying squirrels are active all winter, but you've probably never seen one because they're nocturnal. Unlike their cousins the gray squirrels, flying squirrels rarely come down to the ground. These cute little tree rodents are omnivores, but when insects and birds' eggs aren't available in winter, they subsist on the normal squirrel fare of seeds and nuts. Leave a feeder out at night and spread some peanut butter on a nearby tree trunk. Then watch and wait for them to glide in for a treat.

Weasels, Mink and Fishers

All three of these critters belong to the mustelid family. These cousins range from the least weasel, weighing less than two ounces, to the fisher, which can weigh more than 10 pounds. The most common is the long-tailed weasel, found across the country. Mustelids are pretty elusive, especially northern species of least and long-tailed weasel, both of which sport white fur in the winter. But if you're patient, observant and lucky, you might see one, especially if you have brush piles in your yard. Look for tracks in the snow.

Hawks and Owls

Many hawk species are migratory. Some, however, such as red-tailed hawks, stick around all winter. You can spot them perched in deciduous trees that have lost their leaves. Look for them in the treetops scanning the ground for small mammals and other birds to prey on.

Unlike hawks, many owls are not migratory. Great horned, barred and screech-owls can be easier to spot in bare trees. Some species, however, do migrate, and your only chance of spotting them is in the winter. Both long-eared and northern saw-whet owls may migrate some distance south in fall, and could possibly show up in your backyard. Both like to roost in dense stands of evergreens.

Praying Mantises

You won't find any adult mantises in winter, but they've left signs of life behind. Like many insects, these garden predators die off when there's a freeze, but the next generation lives on in egg cases that were laid the previous summer or fall. Praying mantis egg cases are fairly large and easy to spot: They look like scraggly gray table tennis balls attached to old wildflower or grass stems, or the twigs of trees and shrubs. As soon as the weather warms in spring, the eggs hatch, and hundreds of miniature mantises disperse to begin hunting.

Owls like this great horned are easier to spy in bare trees.

Look for flying squirrels at night

Winter Wildlife ID
Check for these signs of wildlife in your backyard.

TRACKS. Look for footsteps in the snow or mud. Snap a picture and use a track field guide or website to help identify them.

CHEW OR BITE MARKS. Deer, rabbits, beaver and other wildlife each leave distinctive bite marks on the plants they eat.

SOUNDS. Learn the songs, calls or yelps made by songbirds, owls and even mammals like foxes to help you figure out what's nearby.

Feeding Birds in Winter

Battle the cold with these clever backyard feeding tips from our readers.

1

Before the ground freezes, I move the feeders closer to the house, trees and shrubs so the birds are more protected from the wind. I also make sure to keep the suet feeders full. When we're done with our Christmas tree, we stand it up in the snow to provide more protection.
Jennifer Henderson
GALESVILLE, WISCONSIN

2

Be aware of the kinds of birds in your area, and try different seed mixes to see what you can attract. Also, give up trying to keep the squirrels away. Just buy extra feed—the extra entertainment is free!
Danny Redd
GALAX, VIRGINIA

3

When it's snowy, I get out a mini screwdriver and make sure all the feeder holes are free of snow. I also have two heated birdbaths that I keep clean and full all winter long.
Carol Liddy
MILLINGTON, NEW JERSEY

4

I gather large pinecones and fill them with peanut butter and birdseed; then I hang them in the nearby trees. Another trick is using my birdbaths for seed. If it snows, I just throw the seeds on top of the snow.
Marylyn Keene
THOMASVILLE, NORTH CAROLINA

5

During the winter, I keep my feeders full, put out a heated birdbath and offer dried mealworms so the birds have protein.
Julie Zdrazil
CHAMPLIN, MINNESOTA

TOP 10
plants for waxwings

Make your landscape more
appealing to these lovely birds
with a few key plants.
BY MELINDA MYERS

TOP 10

|||||||||||||||||||||||||||||

Every garden should have waxwings! With a little planning, you can lure these gorgeous birds, which travel in flocks, with colorful fruit-bearing plants. Remember that several of these choices are edible, so you might want to plant extras. That way, there will be plenty for you and the birds. The only thing left to do is walk through your landscape and find a space for these bird-friendly plants.

▲ Strawberry
FRAGARIA, ZONES 3 TO 10

The flowers attract butterflies while the fruit brings in waxwings and other fruit-loving birds. Watch for the beautiful red leaves in fall. June-bearing varieties produce one bumper crop per season. If you want several crops, try growing day-neutral or everbearing varieties.

Why we love it: There's always room for strawberries because you can grow them in the ground, hanging baskets or container gardens.

▲ Winterberry
ILEX VERTICILLATA, ZONES 3 TO 9

The red berries of this deciduous holly brighten gray or snowy winter landscapes. Be sure to plant at least one male for every five female plants so there's fruit for the waxwings to feast on. Combine winterberry with evergreens and ornamental grasses for a pleasing winter scene. The plant tolerates wet acidic soils.

Why we love it: A few berry-covered branches will do wonders for your winter container gardens.

◄ Juniper
JUNIPERUS, ZONES 2 TO 9

From tall and slender to low and spreading, juniper comes in a wonderful variety of shapes. The prickly evergreen needles provide shelter, while the berrylike cones offer food for the birds. Needles can be green or bluish-green and may be tipped in white or yellow. Some turn bronzy-purple for winter, while others remain green to brighten the landscape.

Why we love it: There's at least one type of juniper that will grow in just about any part of the world.

▲ Serviceberry

AMELANCHIER, ZONES 3 TO 9

Also know as juneberry or shadbush, this four-season beauty provides white flowers in spring, fruit in June and great fall color. When the leaves drop, they reveal beautiful smooth gray bark. Both tree and shrub forms are available in average heights of 3 to 25 feet.

Why we love it: You can enjoy this edible fruit, too. It tastes like a nutty blueberry.

▲ Hawthorn

CRATAEGUS, ZONES 3 TO 8

Include these small-scale plants in mixed borders, mulched beds or near other plantings where their beauty can shine but you're protected from the thorns. Or select one of the thornless varieties for use near pathways and children's play areas. Hawthorn's white flowers are pretty to look at (but not to smell), and its drought tolerance makes it a good addition to water-wise gardens.

Why we love it: The fruit-laden horizontal branches are breathtaking in winter.

▲ Crabapple

MALUS, ZONES 3 TO 9

Everyone loves crabapple's lightly fragrant white, pink to rosy-red spring flowers, but consider the colorful fruit, too, when choosing one. Look for fire blight- and scab-resistant varieties to increase the beauty and reduce maintenance.

Why we love it: There are so many choices! Upright, weeping and spreading forms are available with yellow, orange or red fruit.

▲ Madrone

ARBUTUS MENZIESII, ZONES 7 TO 11

You may know this broadleaf evergreen for its elegant form and reddish-brown bark, but the waxwings know madrone for the reddish berries. The dark green leaves make a striking backdrop to the white flowers. Plant it in a mixed border or mulch bed to minimize leaf and blossom cleanup. It prefers warm, dry locations.

Why we love it: Madrone's berry clusters may include red, orange and yellow fruit at the same time.

▲ Mountain ash

SORBUS, ZONES 2 TO 6

The North American native and European mountain ashes are small-scale trees that work well in mixed borders and less-than-spacious landscapes. Mulch the soil to keep the roots cool and moist. Proper care is critical to keeping this tree free of pests and looking its best.

Why we love it: Your extra effort in caring for this plant will pay off when the flock of waxwings feasts on the fruit in fall or early winter.

▲ Elderberry

SAMBUCUS, ZONES 3 TO 9

The fragrant white flowers add a bit of aromatherapy to the garden, while the fruit attracts the birds. Include elderberries in your shrub plantings and perennial gardens, or use this suckering plant to help stabilize slopes and riverbanks. Regular pruning will keep it looking its best.

Why we love it: If you have any berries left after the birds get their fill, you can use them to make your own jam, jelly or wine.

▲ Raspberry

RUBUS, ZONES 2 TO 11

Yes, raspberries are delicious, but share some with the waxwings! These vigorous plants make a great hedge, screen or barrier plant in the garden. Proper pruning will increase productivity and reduce pest problems.

Why we love it: Summer- and fall-bearing varieties guarantee that you and the birds will have plenty of delicious fruit to enjoy.

Beware of invasives!

Some berry-producing plants should be avoided. As birds eat the berries, they distribute the seeds in nearby natural spaces. Then the aggressive plants sprout, grow and crowd out native plants. These berry plants have been reported invasive in many areas:

1. Buckthorn
2. Non-native honeysuckle
3. Japanese barberry
4. European cranberry bush viburnum
5. Mulberry
6. Smooth sumac

Feeders for All

You can never have too many bird feeders. Consider these different styles, and try adding a new one to your yard.

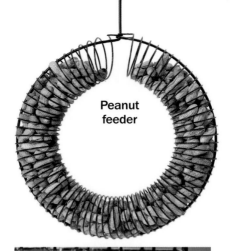

Peanut feeder

Thistle

Often tube-shaped, a thistle feeder holds the small, thin, needle-like seed of the thistle plant (nyjer), which goldfinches love. Sizes range from a simple net bag to metal mesh versions that are several feet long and capable of accommodating dozens of goldfinches.

Tube

Not for nyjer, these tube feeders have holes for larger seeds like sunflowers and safflowers. Look for tube feeders with a weighted contraption that closes off seed access when larger birds or squirrels land.

Suet

You can find more than half a dozen suet feeders on the market, including the classic cage design to hang or a cage attached to a vertical platform, giving woodpeckers a natural perch using their tails as stabilizers.

Log

You can't get thriftier than taking an old log and drilling holes in the side. These holes are perfect for suet or straight peanut butter. Plus, the log gives woodpeckers and other birds a built-in perch.

Peanut

They are usually shaped like a tube, but you can also find peanut feeders in round, wreath shapes. These have large holes, so the birds (and sometimes squirrels) have to work to get the peanuts out.

Sugar-Water

You can find these feeders in a few standard shapes, and they're for those glorious little fliers we call hummingbirds. A second feeder in orange will also attract orioles and other birds—and may discourage ruby-throats from getting territorial over food sources.

American goldfinches on tube feeder

Hopper

The classic hopper is commonly in the shape of a house or a barn, with the seeds feeding down along the long sides. Some come with suet feeders on either end. While a hopper typically doesn't keep squirrels away, it is a surefire way to offer black-oil sunflower seeds to birds of all sizes.

Tray

These hang from a hook or sit atop posts on the ground. Both versions are completely open, so birds have a big space to land and eat. Tray feeders are often used for larger birds like juncos or mourning doves. Squirrels like them, too. Some people who enjoy attracting squirrels put out corncobs on tray feeders.

Downy woodpecker at suet feeder

Ruby-throated hummingbirds at sugar-water feeder

Baltimore oriole at fruit feeder

Fruit

You can find a handful of other feeders on the market, including those that hold fruit like grapes, jelly, oranges and apples. These are great feeders to experiment with, especially in spring and fall, when you'll see the most migrants.

BACKYARD TIP Suet cages aren't just for suet. You can put nesting material in them or try Tip 1 from Richele.

Feeding Innovations

Check out these reader tips for jazzing up your backyard feeder menu.

1

I place fruit slices in my suet basket. The woodpeckers enjoy the special snack, and the basket works perfectly.
Richele Herigan
HARRISBURG, PENNSYLVANIA

2

Birds really enjoy hickory nuts. All you have to do is find a way to break the hickory nuts' rock-hard shells. I hold them steady using pliers, then hit them with a hammer (while wearing safety goggles) and place the broken pieces—shells and all—in my feeders. The birds pick out the meats.
Kenneth Searfoss
READING, PENNSYLVANIA

3

Pecans are a favorite of the birds in my yard. Since these nuts are expensive, I only put out leftovers that have lost their fresh taste. I put a handful in a mesh bag and hang it from a tree limb. It doesn't take long for the birds to find their treat.
Mary Westmoreland
SNYDER, TEXAS

4

When using egg whites, don't throw out the yolks. Scramble them, cool and put them in your feeder. It gives the birds extra calcium.
Nancy Spear
GILFORD, NEW HAMPSHIRE

5

I've fed birds suet blocks for many years, but a less expensive way to satisfy their suet appetite is to simply spread lard on the bark of trees. They love it, and it's a fun way to watch them.
Bruce Schaffner
COCHRANE, WISCONSIN

Berries for Birds

With a little strategic planning, you can use plants to bring in a bevy of fliers.

PLAN AHEAD
Before you dive in and buy several trees or shrubs that may or may not work for your backyard, do a little planning. How big is the space? Do you have an abundance of sun or shade? Determine your specific requirements and bring a list with you to the garden center.

GO NATIVE
It's always best to go native, especially when it comes to berries. Think about it: Birds have been surviving throughout the winter for centuries with food sources readily available in the wild. So it makes sense to consider trees and shrubs in your area that have been mainstays for birds for years. Find a good native plant group or resource for your state or region. It's definitely worth it.

TIME TO RESEARCH
This one is fun. You can pick up a book dedicated to wildlife gardening at a bookstore or the library, but even better—explore on your own. Check out great gardens in your area, including public gardens, botanical gardens and neighbors' yards. When you see a shrub or tree with berries that you like, ask about it.

PLANT RECOMMENDATIONS
Dogwood
Elderberry
Serviceberry
Viburnum
Juniper
Holly
American bittersweet
Beautyberry
Winterberry
Chokeberry
Crabapple
Hawthorn

DID YOU KNOW?
You can attract these berry-lovers: American robins, cedar waxwings, chickadees, eastern bluebirds, gray catbirds, tufted titmice, northern mockingbirds, northern flickers.

Carolina chickadee on hawthorn

All About Oranges

Attract orioles and other birds with these sweet citrus fruits.

IDEAL ORIOLE HABITAT
Plant shrubs, nectar plants and fruit-bearing trees to make your backyard more attractive to orioles. Try crabapple, raspberries, native honeysuckle and trumpet vine.

Nothin' Fancy

Perhaps one of the best things about oranges is the low maintenance. You don't need a snazzy feeder. Simply hammer a nail to a deck railing or fencepost and stick an orange half to the nail. Or set a couple of orange halves right in your platform feeder. Easy peasy!

Early Bird Gets the Orange

Try to anticipate when orioles will arrive in your backyard. You'll have the best chance of success if you put oranges out early. If orioles heading north find a good feeding spot, they may just stick around for breeding season and beyond, which means oriole guests for the entire summer.

Keep it Clean

As you can imagine, fresh fruit spoils quickly, especially in the spring and summer sunshine. Make sure to clean your fruit feeders every few days, remove moldy remains and replace with a fresh batch.

More Fruit Options

Don't stop at oranges. Birds who enjoy a sweet orange treat will often eat other ripe fruit, too. Put out apple halves the same way as oranges. Set an overripe banana, a couple of handfuls of grapes or even chunks of melons on a platform feeder and have fun watching which birds fill up on fruit.

READER SNAPSHOT

As soon as I see the orioles come in, I put out oranges and grape jelly right away. (I don't like to put anything out too early.) Last year, the orioles stayed all summer and I was going through at least one or two oranges per day!
Rebecca Granger
BANCROFT, MICHIGAN

EXPERT ADVICE

"If you're offering fruit for birds, you might attract bonus winged visitors. Some butterflies and moths are attracted to fruit, too!"
Kimberly Kaufman

B&B TIP

Orioles tend to steal the show in the backyard because of their bright colors, but other birds like oranges, too. Look for these less showy birds that might stop for a citrusy snack:

- Gray catbirds
- Northern mockingbirds
- Red-bellied woodpeckers
- Western tanagers
- Brown thrashers
- Scarlet tanagers
- Rose-breasted grosbeaks

Meet the
Native Bees in Your Backyard

Plant your garden with bees in mind and help these powerful pollinators thrive.

BY HEATHER LAMB

Solitary bee

In the world of bees, honeybees get a lot of attention and right now, massive numbers of honeybees are disappearing. This phenomenon, known as colony collapse disorder, threatens both beekeeping operations and the pollination of crops and natural landscapes.

Although colony collapse doesn't impact native bees (honeybees originated in Europe), the possible causes behind colony collapse, such as pesticide use, habitat loss and disease, easily could.

Native bee populations are seeing declines, though not as widely documented as those of honeybees, says Mace Vaughan, co-director of the Pollinator Conservation Program of the Xerces Society. Among native bumblebees, 30 percent of species have experienced significant drop-offs that could lead to extinction.

Concern about colony collapse has brought attention to the critical pollination role of *all* bees and their plight, and also spotlighted what people can do to help, says David Mizejewski, a naturalist with the National Wildlife Federation.

To create a yard that's safe and attractive to native bees, it's important to understand them first. Here are four facts about native bees to help you grow a garden fit for these powerful pollinators.

1. They hide in plain sight.
Native bees can look different from how we often visualize these flying insects. "Most of the things we learn about bees as kids aren't true about native bees," David says. They exist in an array of colors, including metallic green, brown, black and gray, as well as the stereotypical yellow-and-black stripes. Native bees can be quite small and are often mistaken for flies.

It's also useful to note that native bees tend to be docile. "Many can't sting humans," says Heather Holm, the author of *Pollinators of Native Plants*. "Their stingers can't even pierce our skin."

All bees are being threatened right now, including honeybees and native bees.

Bumblebee

Bumblebee

2. To find where they nest, look down.
Most solitary bee species nest in the ground; the rest use tunnels like hollow stems or burrow into dead wood. Inside these nesting sites, the female bee creates a pollen loaf, lays a single egg on it, then starts a new nesting site and repeats the process.

To create a safe habitat for this type of nesting, it's essential to have areas of undisturbed and loose ground. Bees tend to select south-facing slopes with well-drained soil, which can be warmer and drier, and make for good nesting sites. Heather suggests forgoing mulch in spots where you'd like to see bees nest. "Many of the bees are small and can't get through a layer of mulch," she says.

When cutting back your plants in fall, leave behind foot-long lengths of pithy or hollow stems for the tunnel nesters; cavity-nesting bees will also use those stems the next year. You can also create natural bee houses by bundling together hollow stems and hanging them in the yard. Fallen wood, brush piles or old fence posts also provide good nesting sites.

We rely on bees to pollinate flowers like this one and all of our food crops.

Sweat bee

3. Native bees are really busy—help them out.

Most female native bees are active as adults for two to six weeks. During that time, they are collecting pollen to create as many loaves and lay as many eggs as possible. To make foraging for pollen less arduous, provide a diverse selection of flowers from spring to fall and plant them in groups.

New generations and different species of bees are emerging throughout the growing season and it's essential that they have enough flowers for pollen collection. Heather advises gardeners identify flowering gaps during the growing season and add plants to the yard accordingly. "Bees need that continuous succession of plants flowering," she says.

If possible, plant flowers in masses about three feet across. "As bees are flying across a landscape, a cluster of flowers has a billboard effect," Mace says. "It's also efficient, allowing bees to visit many flowers rapidly."

4. Yes, native flowers are best.

The relationship between bees and flowers is symbiotic—bees need the flowers for nectar and pollen, and flowers need the bees for pollination.

Honeybee

Top 10 plants bees love

Create an ideal habitat for bees by planting flowers they need to thrive.

1	Catmint	6	Borage
2	Calendula	7	Foxglove
3	Bee balm	8	Crocus
4	Sedum	9	Anise hyssop
5	Lavender	10	Heliotrope

A flower might be specialized to allow pollination only from certain species of bees, or its structure might help assure proper pollination, Heather says. For instance, if nectar is deep in a flower, a bee will have to push its way into the flower to get at it. For a large, strong bee, like a bumblebee, this is an easy task and the flower deposits pollen on the bee in the process. A smaller bee might not be able to get to the nectar and will seek another flower.

Bring in a hybridized flower, like a cultivar that will display double blooms or a different color, and who knows what effect that change might have on its pollen or nectar. "When we select cultivars of native plants, we don't know how that is affecting other attributes of the flowers that are important to pollinators and wildlife," David says.

In the name of attracting bees, it's best to choose heirloom plants or those bred as little as possible. For ideas, stroll through your local garden center and see which plants are covered with bees, Mace says. Some of the flowers he recommends are anise hyssop, bee balm, catmint, milkweed, penstemon, sedum and sunflower. But depending on the conditions in your yard, there are hundreds that will work. (Find plant lists for different regions at *xerces.org*.)

"The point is that everybody can do something for the bees and everybody can have something pretty," he says. "Plant the right flowers and avoid pesticides. Do that and you'll be rewarded."

Honeybee

Honeybee

Bee garden basics
When gardening for bees, here are a few general rules of thumb:

- **Choose a range of flower shapes and colors to attract the most bee species. Bumblebees can easily collect pollen from complex flowers, while smaller bees appreciate simple flower shapes and a flat place to land.**
- **Plant season-long blooms to support bees from early spring until fall.**
- **Provide areas of undisturbed ground or vegetation for nesting sites.**
- **Bees and flowers have evolved in tandem, so choose non-hybrid natives.**
- **Plant in masses for efficient pollen collection. Sunny areas are most attractive.**
- **Avoid pesticide use. Even some organic mixtures can harm insects.**
- **Provide a muddy area or shallow trough for water.**

Just Add Water

Install a pond and watch your backyard come alive. **BY DAVID MIZEJEWSKI**

Water is the true magnet for attracting wildlife to your yard. While a simple birdbath will do the trick, there's something compelling about the beauty of a backyard pond. When creating a pond, there are several things to keep in mind to make it both attractive and safe for the wildlife.

Think About Size
The size of your pond will influence the kinds of wildlife it will attract. Large ponds offer habitats to wading birds such as herons, egrets and a wide range of waterfowl from mallards to wood ducks. If the pond has large trees along the banks, these birds might even nest there.

While these birds need large, naturalistic ponds, smaller water gardens will also attract some amazing animals. Amphibians such as frogs, toads and salamanders will use nearly any pond as their primary habitat and as a place to engage in courtship, mating and egg-laying. Their tadpoles will grow and complete their metamorphosis in these ponds before dispersing as miniature versions of the adults.

Similarly, dragonflies will use a pond as a nursery for their aquatic larvae as well as their own personal hunting grounds. Even better, amphibians and dragonflies are voracious predators of mosquitoes.

Consider Shape and Depth
The shape of your pond is more of an aesthetic decision than one that will impact wildlife. If you want a natural look, create a pond with an organically curving shoreline, but if you'd like something more formal, go for a linear shape, like a fully

Green darner dragonfly

Bullfrog

rectangular pond. Your backyard wildlife won't mind either way.

Where shape is critically important is in the slopes of the banks. Ponds with steep sides can easily become traps for wildlife that get in but can't get back out. For a pond to be safe, it must have gently graded sloping banks, at least at one end, to create a shallow area where wildlife can enter and exit with ease. An added bonus is that songbirds will use the shallow area to drink and bathe, just like they would a birdbath.

Your pond should be a minimum of two feet at its deepest point, and deeper in areas with colder winters. This not only offers more water volume (and therefore a larger habitat), but it also ensures that fish, tadpoles and hibernating frogs and turtles can safely overwinter without the pond freezing to the bottom.

Plants and Pumps

Always add plants to your pond. Plants filter nutrients out of the water and shade out algae. Native water lilies, rushes and wetland wildflowers add beauty as well as food and cover for wildlife. Add a pump to circulate the water—maybe even power a waterfall—and you'll have a stunning backyard water feature for both you and the wildlife to enjoy!

blooming Beauty

Flowers are the jewels of any garden. Here you'll find our top picks for adding beauty and color to your surroundings, expert advice for keeping plants strong and resilient, and great ideas for gorgeous blooms.

TOP 10
award-winning plants

These brand-new plants received
top honors from the All-America
Selections judges.
BY KIRSTEN SWEET

TOP 10

|||||||||||||||||||||||||||||||||||||||||||||||

1 PETUNIA
2 ANGELONIA
3 OSTEOSPERMUM
4 PENSTEMON
5 ZINNIA
6 GERANIUM
7 SALVIA
8 CANNA
9 CONEFLOWER
10 IMPATIENS

Instead of our annual debut plant list,

we wanted to give you some plants you can get your hands on right now! Rest assured, these plants are still fresh additions to the gardening world, as most were introduced in 2013 and 2014. Each one is an award-winner crowned by All-America Selections, a nonprofit that tests new varieties and introduces only the best performers to the industry as winners. So head to the garden center and start experimenting with some of these newbies.

▲ African Sunset petunia

PETUNIA X HYBRIDA, ANNUAL

Love bright colors? Then this one's for you! African Sunset is one of the first true orange petunias grown from seed. The All-America Selections judges gave it rave reviews for both its stunning color and garden performance.
Why we love it: Gardeners often struggle with petunias, but this one is known for growing evenly and uniformly, with a wealth of season-long blooms.

▲ Serenita Pink angelonia

ANGELONIA ANGUSTIFOLIA, ANNUAL

You might know angelonia as summer snapdragon. Serenita Pink will grow to be about a foot tall and goes well with other outdoor plants. Put this pretty pink stunner in a mixed container or among other soft-hued plants in the landscape.
Why we love it: Requiring very little maintenance, this angelonia is a superb option for beginning gardeners. Don't worry if you forget to water it every once in a while—it's drought-tolerant!

◀ Akila Daisy White osteospermum

OSTEOSPERMUM ECKLONIS, ANNUAL

With a classic daisy shape, bright white color and yellow center, this osteospermum is a real showstopper. It gets high praise for surviving summer heat, even in the South.
Why we love it: Once established, it's drought-tolerant and a really easy, low-maintenance annual.

4

▲ Arabesque Red penstemon

PENSTEMON HARTWEGII, ZONES 6 TO 9

This is the first penstemon to be an All-America Selections winner! The committee even goes so far as to say it's "essential for your garden." For a continuous show of red and white blossoms, simply shear off any spent flowers.

Why we love it: The bell-shaped blooms are very attractive to hummingbirds and butterflies throughout the warm summer months.

6

▲ Pinto Premium White to Rose geranium

PELARGONIUM X HORTORUM, ANNUAL

Good news! It's not necessary to remove the spent blooms on this geranium. New blooms will quickly cover old ones, making this the perfect garden addition for any laidback gardener.

Why we love it: Five-inch, long-lasting blooms. Need we say more? The petals start off white and deepen to pink as the flowers mature.

5

▲ Profusion Double Hot Cherry zinnia

ZINNIA X HYBRIDA, ANNUAL

From spring to frost, this gorgeous zinnia will impress you with deep rose, double-petal blooms. Like others in the Profusion series, Double Hot Cherry isn't picky. In fact, it's easy to grow, will perform well in a wide range of climates and is disease-resistant.

Why we love it: Look for this top performer in a pink-orange color called Profusion Double Deep Salmon.

7

▲ Summer Jewel White salvia

SALVIA COCCINEA, ANNUAL

A recent 2015 winner, this white salvia is the third in the Summer Jewel series. It's a compact grower, but has an abundance of blooms. Plant it in the sun in containers or small garden beds.

Why we love it: Summer Jewel White salvia blooms about two weeks earlier than other white salvias and those blooms are an excellent magnet for bees, butterflies and hummingbirds.

8

▲ South Pacific Scarlet canna

CANNA X GENERALIS, ZONES 8 TO 11

For the flashiest blooms, plant this canna in full sun. It's a heat lover, so South Pacific Scarlet will perform best in warm, humid climates. It's sure to impress, though, with 4-inch scarlet blooms and heights of over 2 feet.

Why we love it: Unlike other cannas, this variety can grow from seed and bloom the same season. It's also more vigorous and uniform in size than other cannas.

9

▲ Cheyenne Spirit coneflower

ECHINACEA X HYBRIDA, ZONES 4 TO 9

Here's an exciting version of your average coneflower. It blooms in a range of colors, including purple, pink, red, orange, yellow and white. Cheyenne Spirit will bloom in summer and wow you into fall. Plus, expect Cheyenne Spirit to grow about 2 feet tall.

Why we love it: This award-winner has been touted as the quickest, brightest, most resilient coneflower yet.

10

▲ New Guinea Florific Sweet Orange impatiens

IMPATIENS HAWKERI, ANNUAL

The blooms of this impatiens variety are bicolored, ranging from light salmon to deep orange. New Guinea Florific Sweet Orange will add that often-lacking pop of color to shade gardens.

Why we love it: It's resistant to downy mildew, which is a serious problem with other impatiens.

2015 veggie winners

It's not just about the blooms! Here are some AAS award-winning vegetables.

1. Hestia Brussels sprouts
2. Dolce Fresca basil (left)
3. Sandy lettuce
4. Emerald Fire pepper
5. Chef's Choice Pink tomato

a dozen
ways to

Find flowers with interesting shapes like these alliums to make a statement in your garden.

dazzle

Express your inner artist with these easy ideas for the garden.

BY RACHAEL LISKA

Each garden, like the person who planted it, has its own personality. Wild. Romantic. Eccentric. Elegant. But the one thing a garden shouldn't be known for is having a wallflower personality. Garner your garden the attention it deserves with these 12 tips and tricks.

1. Love the "Less is More" Rule. It doesn't take much to make a statement, especially in a small garden. A single specimen tree, a brightly painted obelisk, a piece of stone sculpture—set out simple touches like these in visible or high-traffic areas.

2. Embrace Shapes. Formally sculpted evergreens, the spiky fronds of a yucca or the striking ball of blooms atop an allium are good examples of how shapes can create intriguing focal points. Plant in groupings to make a statement or plot out points around the garden to lead an observer's eye through the space.

3. Wow with Water. There's something about water that speaks to the human soul. Whether it's a quiet corner pond teeming with koi or a bubbling stone fountain among the roses, water is a strong element that can't be overlooked. For the biggest splash, opt for flowing water, like waterfalls and streams. If space or budget is an issue, try smaller items like rain chains or a tabletop waterfall.

Seating creates a welcoming space.

Repurpose a fountain into a bold planter.

4. Master the Art of Unpredictability.
Every corner of your garden is an opportunity to show off your unique sense of style. A wall of planted garden boots or teakettles will stop passersby in their tracks. Try grouping quirky collectibles together. Adorn a single tree with pretty beads and ornaments, hang a salvaged chandelier from a rustic arched arbor, or make a wine bottle tree.

5. Learn to Accessorize.
Instead of smaller elements competing for a viewer's attention, use the right garden accessories to spin harmony out of havoc. It's easy to achieve garden unity with structural elements, like large urns or gazing balls. (Here's your chance to go really big!) Try spacing identical pieces along a pathway or placing them in low-growing beds.

6. Catch a Drift.
Planting in drifts, or swaths of colors or textures, is easier said than done. It requires dedicating large areas to one kind of plant, but the attention-grabbing effect it can have on your garden is worth the work. Mass planting works well alongside pathways and garden bed borders. Good plant candidates include Russian sage, purple coneflower, Moonbeam coreopsis, Autumn Joy sedum, coral bells and ornamental grasses.

7. Offer a Seat.
A garden is lovely to look upon, but adding a bench invites visitors to sit down and soak in its beauty. A small seating area fitted with a couple chairs and a bistro table is all you need to create an outdoor room. Set the space apart from its surroundings with a floor made from pavement, crushed stone or manicured grass. Go a step further by creating living walls with a few large shrubs.

8. Go Big.
Plant a few "garden peacocks"—plants with gorgeous, showy blooms or larger-than-life foliage—and get ready for a parade of "oohs" and "aahs." Best bets? Delphinium for its gorgeous spikes of bountiful blossoms, canna for its bright blooms and tropical-like foliage, hydrangea for its impressive size, and blue hosta for its cool-hued leaves.

9. Create Layers.
Like a good outfit, layering builds interest, but it's important to mix textures and keep the color scheme harmonious. If you're not sure where to start, try planting a screen of dark evergreens, ornamental grass or dense shrubbery of the same variety. In front of that, add a row of plants with contrasting textures that require the same growing conditions. A low-growing bloomer—carpet roses, Walker's Low catmint or dianthus—along the outside border finishes the look.

Water always livens up the backyard.

Plant in large patches to really turn heads.

10. Take a Walk. Give your garden room to breathe by incorporating a bit of green space. Wide pathways, grassy courtyards, natural meadows and labyrinths generate an open-air feel. Plus, showier plants really shine when edging an unassuming strip of space.

11. Be Bold with Containers. Magically make over any space with containers. Think big—urns, tall stainless steel planters and old wheelbarrows. Think colorful—glazed ceramic beauties in cobalt blue, sunset orange and lemon yellow finishes. Think dramatic—plants like red cordyline, angel's trumpet, hibiscus or flowering kale. How you display your container creations can have more impact than what is inside them. Secure your containers to a wall, hang them from a fence or stack them on a ladder.

12. Light Up the Night. Well-placed lighting accentuates our most attractive attributes, and the same is true for your garden. There are many options available when it comes to outdoor lighting, from pathway and accent lighting to deck and pond lights. Spotlight landscape features like trees and plants with interesting foliage, and your garden will look as dapper in the dark as it does in the daytime.

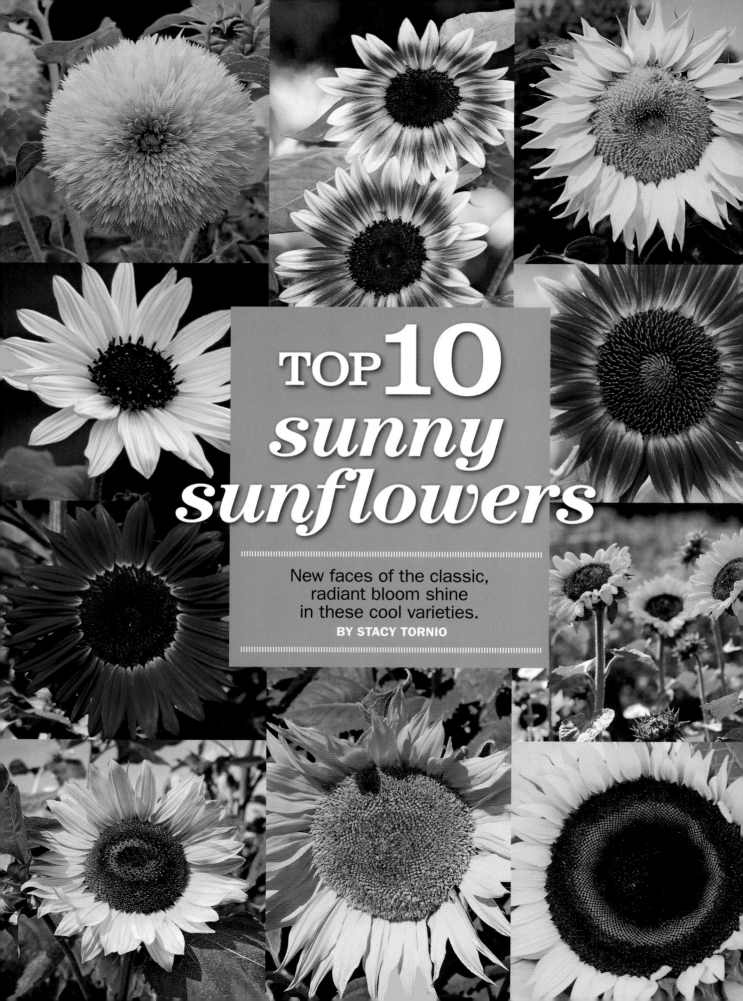

TOP 10 *sunny sunflowers*

New faces of the classic,
radiant bloom shine
in these cool varieties.

BY STACY TORNIO

TOP 10

I've never met a sunflower I didn't like.

They're just so darn cheery and happy—no wonder they're the go-to seed for kids to grow. If you share my love for these big beauties even a little bit, then it's time to start branching out. Sure, the bright yellow blooms that produce seeds for the birds are classics, but there are many more options on the market. It's easy to get overwhelmed by all the cultivars, though, so we're here to help. Start with this list of some of our faves.

▲ Best Double Bloomer
GIANT SUNGOLD

The Teddy Bear cultivar first made double-blooming sunflowers popular—and now you can find even more varieties, including our top pick, Giant Sungold. This plant can easily top 6 feet, while the big puffy blooms grow up to 8 inches wide.

Runner-up: Golden Cheer, which works the shaggy, unkempt look in the best way possible.

▲ Multicolored
STRAWBERRY BLONDE

The petals are rose-pink at the base, while the ends seem to have been dipped in yellow paint. Like most sunflower varieties, Strawberry Blonde grows best in a sunny spot with well-draining soil. This cultivar can grow higher than 6 feet.

Runner-up: Ring of Fire is like an edgier, darker version of Strawberry Blonde. It was also an All-America Selection Winner in 2001.

◀ Best Mammoth
MAMMOTH RUSSIAN

Burpee Home Gardens says if you want to enter a sunflower competition at a fair, this is the one to plant. It grows a whopping 9 to 12 feet tall and produces large striped seeds.

Runner-up: Mammoth Grey Stripe grows 8 to 12 feet tall, with seedheads that are a foot across. Start your seeds early, because they need about 110 days to bloom fully.

▲ Best Light Bloomer
ITALIAN WHITE

You won't find a prettier or more reliable light bloomer. Italian White has a top-notch reputation for dependable 4-inch white blooms with chocolate centers. The plants reach 5 to 7 feet and are known for producing lots of flowers over the course of the season.

Runner-up: Coconut Ice is a newer variety, with petals starting out creamy and then gradually getting lighter.

▲ Dwarf Variety
LITTLE BECKA

Whether you lack space or just like smaller plants, this one should be on your list. At just 3 feet tall, Little Becka packs a big punch, with lots of 6-inch flowers in a unique and vibrant color sequence, from gold to crimson and then back to gold.

Runner-up: Sunny Smile will reach only 12 to 15 inches in height, making it perfect for containers and patios.

▲ Best Dark Bloomer
MOULIN ROUGE

If you like dark, bold sunflowers, this one delivers. You can find other red variations, but Moulin Rouge is the most reliable of the bunch. It grows to about 4 feet tall.

Runner-up: With slightly darker, richer hues than Moulin Rouge, Chocolate is another strong choice and the name says it all.

▲ Award Winner
SORAYA

In 2000, the Soraya cultivar made history when it became the first sunflower chosen as an All-America Selections winner. It boasts stunning blooms on sturdy stems, so you don't have to worry about them falling over. It grows up to 6 feet tall and is a pretty cut flower as well.

Runner-up: Another All-America Selections winner, Suntastic was honored just last year. It's a dwarf and can get up to 20 blossoms on a single plant.

8

▲ Best for Pollinators

LEMON QUEEN

Go online to *greatsunflower.org* and check out the Great Sunflower Project. This group counts pollinators visiting plants, which helps with conservation and plant science. Joining up requires you to plant the No. 1 pollinator around, the Lemon Queen sunflower. We hope you'll sign up to help with the project, but even if you don't, please plant Lemon Queen to support the bee population. As you may have read, bees urgently need our help to survive and keep pollinating plants.

Runner-up: Take your pick! Most sunflowers are good for the bee population, as long as you remember not to pick a pollen-free variety.

10

▲ Best Cut Flower

TAIYO SUNFLOWER

You know those perfect-looking sunflowers you see at grocery stores and flower shops? Chances are they're Taiyos, but you can grow your own cut flowers instead of buying them. These Japanese heirlooms grow 5 to 6 feet tall and have large flower heads with huge centers.

Runner-up: Look for any pollen-free flower to grow for bouquets: It won't make a mess when you bring it indoors (though keep in mind, as mentioned above, it won't benefit bees, either. Try to limit your plantings).

9

▲ Best Sunflower to Eat

SUPER SNACK MIX

Are you growing sunflowers mostly for seed, either for the birds or to munch on yourself? The name says it all for this cultivar. Its originators claim to offer the largest seeds around, which are easy to crack, too. This cultivar grows up to 6 feet and will attract bees and butterflies.

Runner-up: Royal Hybrid is also known for its prolific seed. Remember to let the seedheads dry completely before harvesting.

sunflower sources

It can be hard to find unique or specialty varieties. Here are some of our favorite seed sources.

1. Burpee Home Gardens, *burpee.com*
2. Annie's Annuals & Perennials, *anniesannuals.com*
3. Johnny's Selected Seeds, *johnnyseeds.com*
4. Baker Creek Heirloom Seed Co., *rareseeds.com*
5. Seed Savers Exchange, *seedsavers.org*

healthy plants, happy garden

Stack the odds in your favor by choosing disease-resistant plants that are as breathtaking as they are tough.

BY RACHAEL LISKA

It's early spring,

and you find yourself wandering the aisles of your favorite nursery in hopes of replacing that sickly rosebush you pulled from the garden late last fall. That's when you see it: a robust beauty with emerald-green foliage and a bounty of bright pink blooms. It's picture-perfect. You buy it, plant it and pat yourself on the back for selecting such a fine specimen.

Fast-forward to a beautiful summer day a few months later. You're weeding the garden. And that's when you see them: black spots covering your once-perfect rosebush. Oh, no, not again!

Good Green for Your Green

Now, if you'd planted a Knock Out, New Dawn or Livin' Easy rose instead, you probably wouldn't be in this predicament. Why? Because those cultivars are disease-resistant, friend. That means no black spots and no baby-sitting.

Selecting disease-resistant plants is undoubtedly one of the smartest things you can do when planning or freshening up your garden. Janna Beckerman, extension plant pathologist and associate professor at Purdue University, explains why.

"Plants are selected for a variety of reasons," she says. "Unique flower color, floriferousness and the ability to rebloom are the most obvious. Yet another important but often overlooked trait is disease resistance. A disease-resistant plant is naturally less susceptible to pesky diseases and fungi like leaf spot, blight, gray mold, powdery mildew and rust. These plants are an investment that pays for itself. It also allows you to minimize your use of pesticides."

So what plants tend to be the most vulnerable to disease? "Crabapple, roses, azalea, boxwood, hollyhock, peony, phlox, bee balm, annual and perennial geranium, impatiens, begonia—I could keeping going," Janna says.

Bred to Be Fighters

Plant breeders cultivate new disease-resistant offerings by selecting and crossbreeding plants with the traits they're looking for. Breeding a modest parent plant that is genetically more resistant to disease with a vivacious partner that is known for its big blooms or gorgeous color creates a new variety that boasts the best of both worlds.

Luckily for us gardeners, disease-resistant plants aren't hard to find. Many growers now market them this way, just as they do plants that attract wildlife or tolerate drought. If you still can't find what you're looking for, consider joining one of the many online garden forums on the subject, or check with the experts at your local extension office.

There's an app for that!

Purdue University has several apps designed to help the home gardener diagnose and manage disease and insect problems. Look for the Purdue Perennial Doctor, the Purdue Tree Doctor and the Purdue Annual Doctor. Download them at *purdueplantdoctor.com*.

A few of Janna's personal favorites that work especially well in her neck of the woods (and should throughout the Midwest and Northeast) include Adirondack crabapple, Jacob Cline bee balm, David phlox and both the Pavement and Canadian Explorer series of roses.

There's Power in Prevention

Just as getting enough sleep and exercise help keep human bodies healthy to fight off disease, so do good gardening habits work to keep your plants strong and resilient. The truth is that no plant is 100 percent immune to all disease.

"Sometimes a variety that is resistant in one part of the country could succumb to disease in another area, where the disease pressure is worse because the climate is wetter or warmer," Janna says. "Also, evolution takes place in the garden, just as it does in the outside world, and pathogens can evolve to attack plants that previous generations of disease strains could not."

Janna also notes that geography can mean a lot. For instance, when she goes to California, she notices that the roses have rust problems not common in the Midwest—though Californians don't have to battle black spot nearly quite as much.

The DOs and DON'Ts

Now that you know the benefits of disease-resistant plants, there are a few final things to consider before digging into your flower bed. By following these simple rules, you'll be well on your way to a disease-free garden.

• DO select plants that thrive in your zone. Otherwise, stressful conditions weaken their performance and make them more susceptible to problems.

• DO plant the right plant in the right site, according to its light requirements.

• DON'T crowd your plants, and DO maintain good weed control. Good airflow is critical.

• DO pay attention to the plant's water requirements. Growing bee balm in a dry site makes it susceptible to powdery mildew, while growing iris in a wet area predisposes it to root rot.

• DO water in the morning when the foliage has all day to dry, and DON'T water overhead, which can splash soil—where nasty stuff lurks—onto the foliage.

• DON'T overfertilize. People view fertilizer like vitamins—something that keeps living things healthy. But too much can be a bad thing, which can actually make plants more susceptible to disease.

Disease-Resistant Dynamos

1. Aster, New England – **Harrington's Pink**, Honeysong Pink, Purple Dome

2. Azalea – Darlin's Dream, **Flame Creeper**, Sautee Sunset

3. Bee Balm – Jacob Cline, **Pardon-My-Pink**, Gardenview Scarlet

4. Begonia – Duarten, Marion Louise, Pauline, Peace, **Vesuvius**

5. Geranium, Perennial – Alan Bloom, Buxton's Blue, Biokovo, **Rozanne**

6. Impatiens – Bounce, **New Guinea**

7. Peony – America, **Sarah Bernhardt**, Scarlet O'Hara

8. Phlox, Garden – **David**, Laura, Robert Poore

9. Rose – Blaze of Glory, **Golden Showers**, Heart Song, Knock Out, Olympiad, New Dawn

10. Rudbeckia – Cherry Brandy, **Tiger Eye Gold**

11. Speedwell – Icicle, **Crater Lake Blue**, Sightseeing

12. Verbena – Aztec Dark Red, **Coral**, Empress Strawberry, Rapunzel Lilac

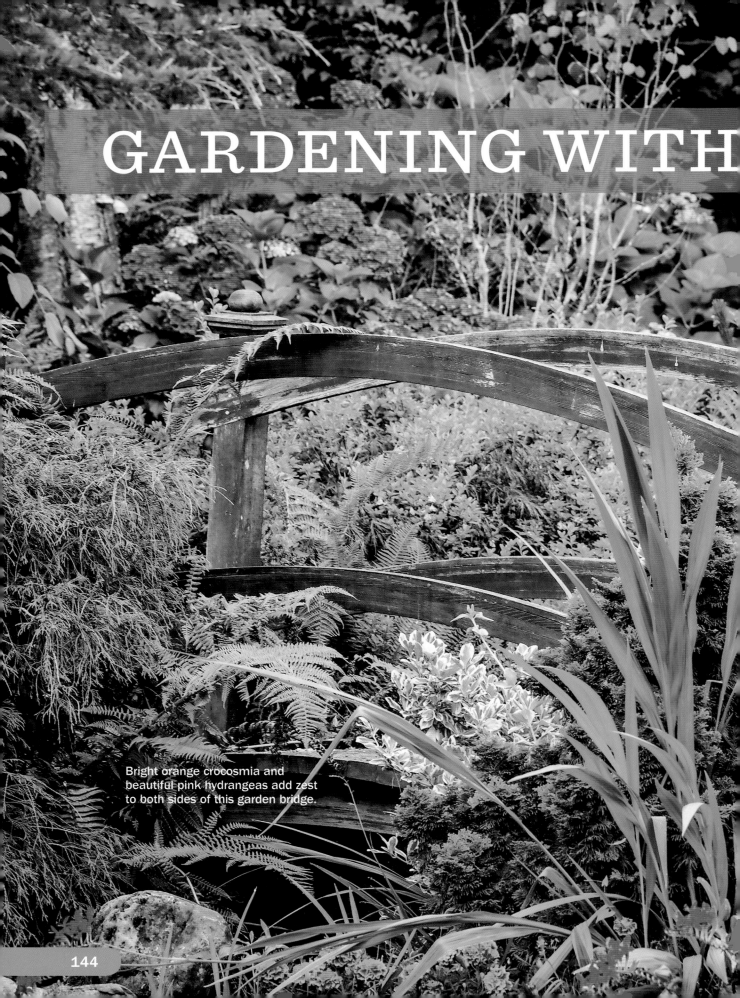

GARDENING WITH

Bright orange crocosmia and
beautiful pink hydrangeas add zest
to both sides of this garden bridge.

COLOR

Plant the right hues to create a warm and inviting backyard space.

BY TAMMI HARTUNG

The white veronica adds brightness among purple salvia.

Gardens are the essence of color.

Visitors will experience a garden differently depending on what color scheme the flowers and foliage create. They may find it tranquil or invigorating, simply because of how the garden's colors work together. Wildlife visitors are drawn to color, too. With the right hues, you can invite birds, butterflies and more to your backyard. Ready for your lesson in color? Let's begin!

Cosmos

Embrace the Classics

Blues, purples and pinks are favorites for gardeners. For some beautiful purple and blue flower options, look to lavender, campanulas, salvia and lupines. Equally nice are pink blooms like purple coneflowers, cosmos, and hollyhocks. Don't overdo it, though. Flowers in the purple, pink and blue color range give the garden a lovely watercolor look, which can have a very peaceful and relaxing effect on visitors strolling along the garden path. However, stand back 10 feet or more from the garden, and it's a completely different effect. The colors tend to blend together so well that the garden loses much of its definition. Onlookers will see only a bluish or pinkish blur.

Add Contrast

To break up your pink and purple garden, you'll want to look to the next color grouping—oranges, reds and yellows. These shades create an atmosphere that is invigorating, uplifting and feisty! Choosing plants like black-eyed Susans, poppies, zinnias and Mexican sunflowers will make you feel happy and energized in no time.

Many of those warm-colored flowers will also welcome pollinators and birds to the garden. For example, butterflies can't resist the bright blooms of sunflowers and butterfly weed. Nearly every red tubular flower, like penstemon or salvia, will attract hummingbirds, and Mexican sunflower seeds are irresistible to goldfinches and other seedeaters.

The No Color Rule

You might not think of white flowers as a colorful garden staple, but they are. Including enough white flowering plants and those with silver-gray foliage is an important aspect in planning any garden. Strive for a garden that has 30 percent of its plants falling in this category.

White flowers or silver-gray foliage brighten up the garden, giving it a fresh look. This is especially important in the heat of summer or at the end of the season when the garden begins to take on a tired look. If you have some white baby's breath or chamomile planted throughout the garden, their white blooms will add a cheerful touch. The same thing happens when woolly lamb's ears, Greek mullein and gray santolina are thrown in the mix, because all of them have silver-gray foliage.

Along with other colors, white flowers also attract plenty of beneficial insects. Ladybugs, lacewings, and hoverflies hunt pests like aphids and are just a few of the helpful insects you can expect to find in your garden. Having abundance of these insects in the garden translates to a garden mostly free of pests, so you don't need to rely on the use of pesticides.

Don't Forget Foliage

Finally, embrace color and texture in any garden by taking advantage of different types of foliage. There are many interesting shades of green and gold foliage, as well as purple and red in plants like red rubin basil or shiso. The endless varieties of shapes and textures of the leaves will keep any garden visitor interested in the landscape.

TOP PICKS FOR COLOR

FLOWERS OF PURPLE AND BLUE
1. Catmint 2. Rosemary 3. Verbena

FLOWERS OF PINK
4. Hollyhock 5. Yarrow 6. Rhododendron

FLOWERS OF YELLOW
7. Black-eyed Susan 8. Goldenrod 9. Rue

Mugwort, although invasive in some areas, is a great perennial with red stems and deeply cut leaves, which are green on top and silvery underneath. When a breeze comes, this plant shimmers. Bronze fennel, with bronzy green foliage and yellow flowers, is a tall plant that makes an attractive statement wherever it grows. There's the fine foliage of fountain grass and the leathery feel to tulip or iris leaves. All of these plants create interest, complement flowers and make the garden a true place of beauty.

Variegated foliage is nearly a whole garden world by itself, with a great many variegated thymes, dianthus, oreganos and more. Use a bit of care with some golden variegations in foliage, though, because they sometimes clash if planted next to chartreuse or bright pink flowers. Intermixing variegated foliage with rich solid leaf colors of any shade will make your garden look stunning.

TOP PICKS FOR COLOR

FLOWERS OF ORANGE AND RED
1. Butterfly weed 2. Calendula 3. Jupiter's beard

FLOWERS OF WHITE
4. Phlox 5. Alyssum 6. Shasta daisy

FOLIAGE OF SILVER AND GRAY
7. Helichrysum 8. Gray santolina
9. Woolly lamb's ears

glad you asked!

Gardening expert Melinda Myers answers your questions.

DID YOU KNOW?
Spirea is not a shade-loving shrub. It will tolerate some shade, but performs best in full sun.

◀ Can you tell me the name of this wildflower? It's growing on the eastern side of a hill.
Phaedra Roberts TRION, GEORGIA

This North American native is wild comfrey (*Cynoglossum virginianum*). It's in the same family as borage and forget-me-nots, and you can see similarities in the blooms. You usually find this plant in upland woods, forested wetlands and hardwood or mixed forests in the eastern half of the U.S.

▲ My spirea plants are in full sun and get normal amounts of water. They appear to be turning brown and partially dying. Is water the problem?
Donald Thurlow WHITEHOUSE, TEXAS

Too much and too little water could be the cause. Water thoroughly when the top few inches of soil are dry. Make sure water is draining away, not collecting, around the roots. Use a pipe to remove a plug of soil or carefully dig down near the plant to check drainage. Adjust the amount of water or consider moving the plant to an area with better drainage if needed.

▲ **I transplanted a trumpet vine from a friend's yard that had lots of blooms. My vine has only had one bloom in several years. What's wrong?**
Rose Seely SPENCER, NEW YORK

I know it can be tough, but trumpet vines require patience. First and foremost, they need to reach maturity before they start blooming. This can take several years after planting. It's important to avoid high nitrogen fertilizers, because they promote leaf and stem growth while also preventing flowering. Trumpet vines develop an extensive root system that allows them to absorb nutrients from surrounding plant beds and nearby lawns. This means you need to be careful when

fertilizing these areas. Use a low-nitrogen, slow-release fertilizer to increase your chance of having a beautiful, blooming vine.

Is it safe to put down plastic and red bark chips to keep weeds and grass out of my perennial garden?
Vicki Kloepping KENT, ILLINOIS

A better idea would be to use shredded leaves, evergreen needles or wood mulch directly on the soil in your perennial garden. Plastic barriers can create short-and long-term problems in the garden. When the wood chips covering the plastic break down, they make a layer of compost. The plastic prevents the compost from improving the soil below and creates the perfect growing conditions for weed seeds to sprout and grow. Before long the plastic rips and ultimately allows weeds to grow. Plus, the torn plastic is unsightly.

When I got out my pots from last fall, tons of little bugs with wings covered the old soil. Can I reuse the soil?
Suzanne Foote CAYUGA, NEW YORK

In general it's best not to save and reuse potting mix when the soil or plants are infested with insects or infected with disease. So discard that soil and clean the pots before you use them again. Dip each pot in a solution of 1 part bleach to 9 parts water. Then rinse in clear water and they'll be ready for fresh soil and new plants!

▼ **I was given a small lilac bush years ago from a friend's garden. Every spring I'm so disappointed to see no flowers. How can I get it to bloom?**
Georgette Jahn DINGMANS FERRY, PENNSYLVANIA

Shade and improper pruning can prevent lilacs from flowering. Make sure your plant receives at least six hours of sunlight. If not, consider moving it to a sunnier location. Avoid high nitrogen fertilizer because it can prevent flowering. Only prune lilacs right after their normal bloom period in early summer if you want flowers the following spring. Pruning at other times eliminates the flower buds and your spring bloom.

Can you help me identify this shrub? It has deep red flowers with yellow stamens.
Linda Wright SHIRLEY, MASSACHUSETTS

Your mystery plant is Carolina allspice (*Calycanthus floridus*). It's native from Virginia to Florida and hardy in zones 4 to 9. This suckering shrub grows 6 to 10 feet tall. The plant is adaptable, but for best results, grow in full to part sun and moist, loamy soil. The fragrant spring blooms can be used as cut flowers and the leaves turn a pretty golden yellow in the fall. An extra benefit is that deer tend to leave it alone.

▲ **My amaryllis has five green leaves, and it's about 14 inches tall, but no bloom. What could be wrong with it?**
Joyce LeMaster PHARR, TEXAS

You're lucky to be able to grow amaryllis indoors or out in your area. Start by evaluating the growing conditions. Make sure your plant is in a mostly sunny spot with a bit of afternoon shade and moist, well-drained soil. Avoid excess nitrogen fertilizer, which can prevent flowering. Grow indoor amaryllis plants in a sunny window and water as needed. Consider moving them outdoors spring through summer. In late summer cut back on watering and move the plant to a cool location indoors to induce dormancy. In eight to 10 weeks you should notice new growth. Bring your sprouting amaryllis into a warm, sunny window to encourage growth and flowering.

I found a white substance at the bottom of my red tip (Photinia) plant. It looked like soap suds or mushy snow. After several hours, it disappeared. What was it?
Nick Nicholson WILLIAMSTON, NORTH CAROLINA

It sounds like spittlebugs, also known as froghoppers, were feeding on your red tip. These small insects hide in the substance you saw and suck plant juices. They create the foamy froth by secreting a clear, sugary substance and using their legs as billows. The froth protects the insects from predators and the environment. Control is usually not needed, especially when the populations are small. A strong blast of water is usually enough to dislodge the froth-covered insects and minimize plant damage.

▶ **I have had bear's breeches for over five years. They've multiplied beautifully, but I never get any flowers. Why?**
Cate Mills MIDDLEBUSH, NEW JERSEY

Fortunately, bear's breeches (Acanthus) produce beautiful foliage as well as lovely flowers. Too much shade and high-nitrogen fertilizer can result in poor or no flowering. The fact that your plants are quickly multiplying leads me to believe they may be getting too much nitrogen.

DID YOU KNOW?
Bear's breeches leaves can reach 1 foot wide and 2 feet long.

Consider topdressing the soil with compost every other year, and only using a low-nitrogen, slow-release fertilizer if needed. Too much shade can delay flowering, so be patient or move the plants to a sunnier location if the change in fertilization doesn't do the trick.

FAQ

"How do I use the seeds from a geranium plant to start new plants?"
Elena Vahmenko RUSSEL, IOWA

Keep in mind that the geraniums you buy at the garden center are hybrids, and they're unlikely to come true from seed. That means the seedlings may be a different size or produce different-colored flowers than the original plant. Remove seeds from the pods and store in a cool, dark place. Start them indoors in late winter and be patient. It takes at least three weeks for the seeds to sprout.

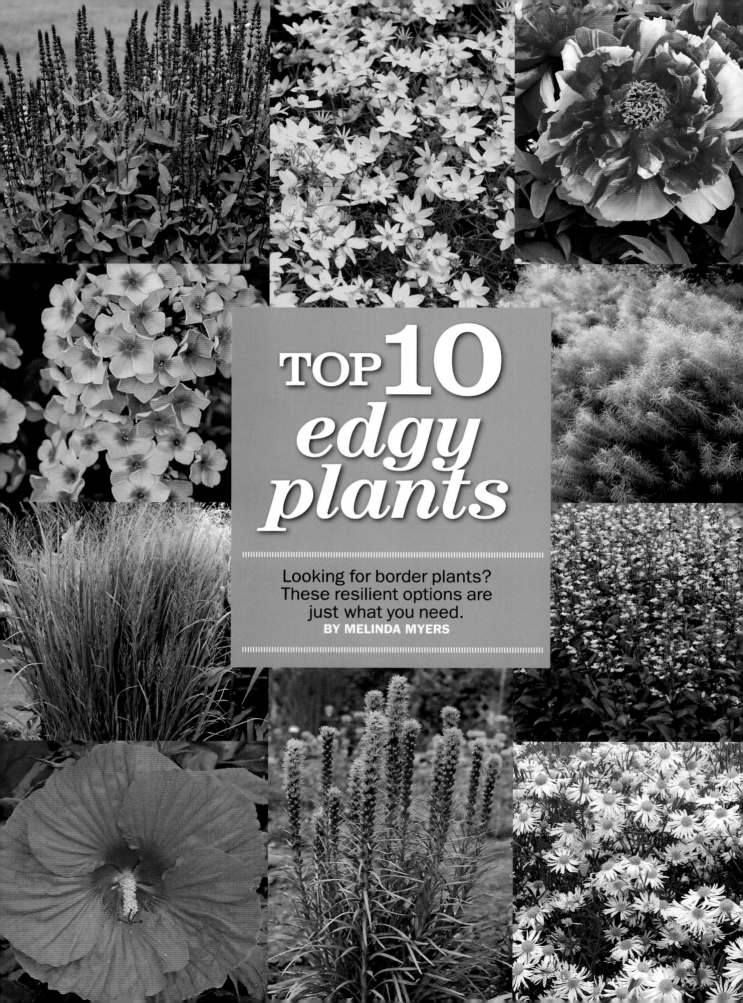

TOP 10 *edgy plants*

Looking for border plants? These resilient options are just what you need.

BY MELINDA MYERS

TOP 10

Never underestimate the value of great border plants. They can dress up a bare fence, create a screen and add a bit of needed color next to your house or shed. For the best results, use a mix of plants. Add options that provide color from spring through fall, and that range in height. In addition, include plants with fine foliage and flowers to contrast with the bold leaves and blooms of neighboring plants. It's time to conquer those edges!

▲ Caradonna salvia
SALVIA NEMOROSA 'CARADONNA,' ZONES 3 TO 9

The fragrant green foliage is topped with spikes of indigo flowers on purple-black stems in early summer. Deadhead faded flowers for additional bloom throughout the summer. Though it prefers full sun and moist, well-drained soil, it will tolerate drought, heat and humidity.
Why we love it: It brings those hummingbirds and butterflies out to the border where we can get a closer look.

▲ Willow amsonia
AMSONIA HUBRICHTII, ZONES 4 TO 9

Light blue, star-shaped flowers top the fine foliage of this spring blooming native, and the leaves seem to glow when they turn yellow-gold in the fall. You'll have the best results growing this 3-foot tall plant in full sun. Avoid shade and over fertilization because it can lead to floppy growth.
Why we love it: It's drought-tolerant once established, and the deer tend to let it be.

◀ Peony
PAEONIA, ZONES 3 TO 8

Add three seasons of charm with this old-fashioned favorite. Known for their large and often-fragrant flowers, the foliage also provides interest for multiple seasons. Watch as the leaves emerge with a reddish tint in spring, turn deep green for summer and finish off the season with purplish red shade in fall. Select varieties with stiff stems that do not need staking, like buckeye belle.
Why we love it: It's a long-lived, low-maintenance perennial for sunny borders.

▲ Switchgrass

PANICUM VIRGATUM, ZONES 3 TO 9

In late summer the delicate light pink flowers hover above the fine foliage of this tall North American native grass. The yellow fall color and persistent seed heads extend your enjoyment into fall and winter. Select a clump-forming cultivar like Heavy Metal, Northwind or Shenandoah, which are more suitable for the garden.

Why we love it: You'll enjoy the butterflies that visit the flowers and finches that feed on the seeds.

▲ Dark towers beardtongue

PENSTEMON 'DARK TOWERS,' ZONES 3 TO 9

Border plants aren't just for the front of the garden. This tall, summer-blooming perennial will add color and vertical interest to the middle or back of the border. Bicolored bell-shape blooms top the colorful foliage, which hummingbirds will love. Heat, humidity and drought tolerance makes this a good choice for sunny borders.

Why we love it: The reddish-purple foliage color persists throughout the season.

▲ Garden phlox

PHLOX PANICULATA, ZONES 4 TO 8

Great for the middle or back of the border, garden phlox adds color to summer and fall garden borders. The white, pink, red, blue or purple flowers are often fragrant. Select powdery, mildew-resistant varieties, and grow in full sun to light shade and moist, well-drained soil.

Why we love it: You'll enjoy it in so many ways—including as a cut flower. Plus, it lures butterflies and hummingbirds to your garden.

▲ Snowbank false aster

BOLTONIA ASTEROIDES 'SNOWBANK', ZONES 4 TO 8

The large size and fine texture of this plant make it a nice addition to the middle or back of the border. The small, white daisy-type flowers appear late summer through fall. Grow in full sun and well-drained soil for best results and to avoid the need for staking.

Why we love it: The flowers look like a cloud has descended onto your garden. The white blossoms brighten the night and a fall garden.

▲ Zagreb coreopsis

COREOPSIS VERTICILLATA 'ZAGREB,' ZONES 3 TO 9

Brighten the border with a long-blooming coreopsis. The ferny foliage creates a nice backdrop for small daisy-shaped flowers. This short coreopsis makes a great stand-alone edger plant, or tuck it along the front of other border plants for added color. Regular division will keep this perennial blooming with minimal deadheading.

Why we love it: Not all border plants give such reliable color. Yet, these flowers will enliven spaces from early summer all the way through fall.

▲ Hardy hibiscus

HIBISCUS MOSCHEUTOS, ZONES 4 TO 9

The 6- to 12-inch flowers of this back-of-the-border plant will wow you from summer through fall. Grow in full sun to partial shade with moist soil. It is one of the last perennials to emerge in spring. This means you'll want to mark its location with a stake or spring flowering bulbs, so you don't accidentally damage it during spring cleanup.

Why we love it: The plants are tall and make a statement, yet they seldom need staking.

▲ Blazing star

LIATRIS SPICATA, ZONES 3 TO 8

The purple or white spikes of blossoms add vertical interest to the flower garden and cut flower bouquets. Native to moist meadows and marshes, this native perennial prefers full sun and moist, well-drained soil, and it grows up to 4 feet. Select the variety Kobold, if you want more compact plants.

Why we love it: The seed heads provide winter interest and food for the birds.

shrubs for a sunny border

Shrubs make a nice addition to the garden border. Use taller ones as a backdrop, but don't be afraid to mix medium and small shrubs into the perennial flower mix. Here are some to consider.

- Caryopteris
- Ceonanthus
- Daphne
- Deutzia
- Dogwood
- Hypericum
- Lilac
- Mahonia

- Ninebark
- Panicle hydrangea
- Rose of Sharon
- Shrub roses
- Smokebush
- Viburnum
- Weigela

plant 'em &

Add these resilient and reliable plants

BY SALLY ROTH

forget 'em

o your garden this fall.

every gardener dreams of plants they can pop in the ground and enjoy for years to come without a lot of work or maintenance—plants anyone can grow.

It's not too late in the season to add these kinds of plants to your backyard landscape. In fact, it's a wonderful time to score deals on perennials and fill in those bare spots in your garden.

These plants, as long as they are hardy in your region, will adapt to all sorts of soil, from lush loam to clay, and to all kinds of conditions. They look good even when they're out of bloom, lending texture with their handsome foliage. All you need is six hours of sunlight a day. Then, just plant and walk away.

Head to the garden center and buy end-of-the-season salvia, penstemon and pansies to put in the ground now, before frost comes.

Monch aster

Powis Castle artemisia

Splash of Sunshine

Happy yellow flowers will light up any backyard. Start scouting for great daffodils, a bulb celebrated for their resistance to deer, squirrels and other critters. Varieties to look for include King Alfred and Tete A Tete (turn to page 159 to find out where to purchase it).

For a low-maintenance, midseason bloomer, choose Happy Returns daylily. It's a rebloomer that sends up occasional blooms all season and its lemony flowers complement any companion. Plant this downsized daylily in front of beds or among other garden flowers for contrasting foliage.

One of the tallest garden perennials is a cutleaf coneflower. This rugged heirloom is perfect for brightening a privacy fence. Tie garden twine or plant tape around the stems through the fence to help them hold up the fluffy double yellow daisies.

Get the Blues

Veronicas have been garden favorites for years, thanks to their bluest-of-blue color and agreeable disposition. Go for upright growers like Sunny Border Blue or Royal Candles for months of bloom, or plant groundcover types such as Georgia Blue.

Catmint (*Nepeta*) creates a billow of blue that begins at bearded-iris season and keeps going until fall. Look for Six Hills Giant, Walker's Low and Blue Wonder that are better behaved in the garden.

For a dramatic blue-purple color, try May Night or East Friesland salvias. They're perfect partners for white Shasta daisies or pale pink dianthus.

Lavender-blue Monch aster (*Aster x frikartii*) kicks in at the June peak of perennial bloom, much earlier than many asters, and keeps going through the first fall frosts. Hardy geranium Rozanne, whose intense blue will make your jaw drop, blooms the same way. Both are hardy to Zone 5.

Butterfly Banquet

Sedums draw butterflies and bees to their summer flowers. Made for hot, dry places, sedums store water in their leaves. Waterlogged soil is a death knell, but they'll do fine in average conditions, as long as they get plenty of sun. They're perfect for hillside niches among rocks, in gravel or sandy soils, atop walls or along a sidewalk. Hardiness varies, so check the tag.

Autumn Joy and other upright sedums stay in a clump. But ghostly gray Cape Blanco, red Dragon's Blood, chartreuse Angelina and other groundcover types spread rapidly. Choose a spot where their natural habit is an asset, not a drawback—edging your driveway, spilling over a wall or covering a slope—and you won't have to rein in these fast growers.

The variety of colors and leaf shapes, plus the butterfly-attracting flower clusters, make sedums addictive. With dozens of varieties, your only challenge will be not buying them all.

Silver Spotlight

Soft as velvet, lamb's ears spread into a solid patch of silvery leaves. Fuzzy stalks of purplish pink flowers arrive

Lamb's ear

Angelina and Dragon's Blood sedums

Russian sage

Big chief tulip   Tri-color crocus

in early summer, but it's the silver stems and foliage that steal the spotlight. Plant a swath of lamb's ears among other perennials for an eye-catching accent, or use them to edge your beds. Straying stems, which root as they go, are easy to peel up if they spread too far.

The silver foliage of artemisia is a treasure, but the running roots of Silver King or Silver Queen cultivars can take over the garden as soon as you turn your back. For good behavior, you can't beat Lambrook Silver, a filigreed mound that stays in place, and similar but less hardy (to Zone 6) is Powis Castle.

Russian sage (*Perovskia*) was an instant hit when it burst on the garden scene, and its popularity keeps rising. The silvery plant finishes the summer season with an arching fountain of blue flowers that beckon to migrating monarchs and other butterflies.

Green Thumb Club

Year after year, these undemanding perennials keep going. They leave us free to fiddle with fussier plants or experiment with new combinations.

With easy plants as the foundation, your gardening thumb will get greener every day. The best fertilizer for that process? The admiring comments you'll hear from friends and neighbors.

it's time to plant bulbs!

Looking for new bulb varieties? We've chosen a selection of bulbs we love, including three *Birds & Blooms* Editors' Choice picks. Head to *birdsandblooms.com/burpee* to purchase a few of our favorites and get them in the ground this fall.

Tete A Tete daffodil

Summer Container Tip

Freshening up your garden might mean adding a couple of fresh pots. Placing a new container next to old ones can mask the unsightly parts of spring containers. Plus, starting a few additional pots will give your green thumb an extra workout.

potted plant *revival*

It's the second half of summer and things in your container garden might be looking, well, not so great. Give your potted plants a midseason boost with these tips.

BY KIRSTEN SWEET

If you glance out the window and your container garden looks a little lackluster, you're not alone. *Birds & Blooms* garden expert, Melinda Myers, says this is quite common.

"By midseason, some plants fade and get crowded out by more vigorous plants. The bigger ones take off and take over," Melinda says.

Part of this is due to the instinct to pack as many plants as possible into one container when planting in spring. Of course, doing so provides instant gratification, but you're not taking into account that these plants will get bigger, grow large roots in their pots and end up using a lot of space.

Another reason is lack of attention. By August, busy summer schedules cause a lot of people to forget about their pots. This, combined with a mix of hot temperatures, can take a toll on potted plants.

"A lot of plants thrive in warm, but not hot temperatures. When it gets hot, we need to water more often, but by midsummer, we're not as attentive," Melinda says.

Don't worry. We have some easy ways to put a little life back into your small space garden.

Don't Slack on Watering

Those wilting, ragged plants will benefit from a little extra hydration, especially if you're experiencing an extremely hot and dry summer. Here are a couple of tricks to figure out if your pots are in need of a good watering. First, simply lift the pot—if it's really light, give it a hearty drink. Second, stick your finger in the soil. If the top few inches are dry, you'll know that it needs a good soak.

Be generous with the water. It's hard to overwater pots if you have proper drainage holes. Melinda says for best results, check the pots daily, water early in the day and check them again later. You might find they need a second helping of water. The change in weather and increased temperatures can be brutal for potted plants, so staying on top of watering is a simple way to encourage plants to keep performing through the end of summer.

Groom and Feed

Ideally, plant grooming should be done throughout the growing season, but if you haven't kept up with deadheading and trimming, it's definitely not too late to start. Your plants will still benefit from deadheading this late in the season, so it's worth it to take the time to pluck off spent blooms.

Just the basics—trimming long, leggy plants, deadheading and pinching back the plants—can do wonders, even late in the game.

The same goes for fertilizing annuals. Just because you haven't kept up with the chore, doesn't mean it's too late. Some containers need it most in late summer if they're expected to keep up the floral show. Give them a midseason boost with slow-release fertilizer.

Buy New Additions

You might find that all of the watering, deadheading and fertilizing in the world simply won't perk up your plants. There's no shame in throwing in the towel, grabbing a trowel and carefully digging out under-peforming plants and replacing them with new ones.

"If you've tried pruning and it doesn't look like the plant is revivable, replacing it is a good idea," Melinda says. But do this minimally and remove the old plant and its roots to allow space for new additions. Just be careful not to damage the roots of remaining plants.

While the garden center selection won't be as exciting as when you first visited in spring, you'll be able to find some healthy annuals to fill the empty spaces in your pots. Plus, expect to get some great deals.

Melinda says garden centers aren't like they used to be. Now, a trip to the nursery in August will yield many more options, like ready-made containers and fresh batches of plants. "The plants they're selling at this time of year are the ones that are going to thrive for the rest of the season," she says. "Look for things like light, airy grasses. They can help fill in gaps and you won't even be able to tell they were planted three months apart."

Even if you do all of these things, remember that it'll take a week or two for your pots to perk back up. But you'll be rewarded for your efforts with a beautiful late-summer container garden.

Quick Tip
The late summer is a good time to experiment with autumn hues such as gold and purple.

1.

5.

Late-Season Container Plant Picks

Use these beauties for new containers or as additions.

1. Diamond Frost euphorbia
2. Hosta
3. Zinnia
4. Heuchera
5. Summer snapdragon
6. Yarrow
7. Petunia
8. Marigold
9. Lantana

6.

9.

Easy-to-grow coneflowers are one of the most reliable perennials.

Never-Fail Plants

Readers share their resilient, tried-and-true picks for the garden.

1

My purple coneflowers are amazing. They multiply every year, and the hummingbirds and butterflies love them. When they're done blooming, the goldfinches devour the seed. I would not have a garden without them.

Rebecca Way
PARKVILLE, MISSOURI

2

Petunias. I have pots of these in several colors on the front and back porch every summer. They practically grow themselves with little care beyond watering and pulling off the dead blooms. Plus, they were my grandma's favorite, and they always remind me of her.

Tammy Godwin
NEW MARKET, ALABAMA

3

Profusion zinnias. I discovered these a few years ago, and I love them. They reseed each year and are gorgeous. They're great for filling in bare spots in flower beds.

Amy Gupton
CHASE CITY, VIRGINIA

4

I used to think hostas were boring plants. However, gardening in chilly Minnesota has brought me to appreciate them immensely. Any variety survives our long winter. I really believe you can't kill them.

Cindy LaVan
ST. PAUL, MINNESOTA

5

Balloon flower is a perennial favorite of mine. You can divide and move it, and it still flourishes. Bees love it, and it deadheads easily. Plus, it will bloom nearly all summer and into a warm fall.

Susan Steele
LIVONIA, MICHIGAN

did you know?

Ready to celebrate? Learn how flowers and trees make our favorite spring holidays extra special.

66

Most moms—66% of them, according to the National Retail Federation—can expect to receive flowers for Mother's Day this year.

9

In Hawaii, May Day is also known as Lei Day, when a variety of leis are made and exchanged. Each of Hawaii's nine islands has its own official lei.

1872

An estimated one million trees were planted in Nebraska on April 10, 1872—the first Arbor Day celebrated in the U.S.

1967

Before Memorial Day was declared the official name in 1967, this holiday was also known as Decoration Day due to all the flowers placed on soldiers' graves.

1

More than 1 billion people participate in Earth Day every April, from planting trees and flowers to building birdhouses and picking up litter.

7

This year marks the seventh annual National Public Gardens Day. Botanical gardens nationwide organized special events and activities, including free admission.

12

Growers along the California and Oregon border produce 12 million Easter lilies a year. This area is known as the Easter lily capital of the world.

Mimosa
Photo by
Jean Mattingly

Sunflower
Finalist in our Backyard Photo Contest
Photo by Nancy Tully

Queen Anne's Lace
Finalist in our
Backyard Photo Contest
Photo by Cindy Nelson

Tiger Lilies
Finalist in our Backyard Photo Contest
Photo by Pam Lanting

Dahlia
Finalist in our Backyard Photo Contest
Photo by Lisa Richardson

great Escapes

Ignite your wanderlust with an armchair tour of some of the best places in the U.S. and Canada to spot spectacular flora and fauna. Search for the elusive species on your life list. Get travel tips from fellow nature enthusiasts who have visited prime destinations.

BRIAN LASENBY/SHUTTERSTOCK.COM

best birding across *America*

Grab some binoculars and hit the road! Here are 50 of our favorite birding spots—one for every state!

BY KAITLIN STAINBROOK

*W*hat's the No. 1 place in the United States to go birding? It's a tough call. There are classic stops such as Montana's Glacier National Park—the bird-watching trails with mountain backdrops make it worth the visit alone. But there are plenty of hidden gems, too, like the Waikamoi Preserve in Hawaii— the only place in the world where intrepid birders are likely to see Maui parrotbills.

After consulting our travel experts (special thanks to Rob Ripma with Sabrewing Nature Tours), we realized it would be impossible to name just one birding location as our winner. Instead, we picked a top bird-watching destination from every state. (We even squeezed in a couple of Canadian sites.)

Think of this as your official invitation to get out there and explore new places!

ATLANTIC PUFFIN

Kenai Fjords
National Park,
Alaska

Alabama
Dauphin Island

As cold fronts move southward, bringing rain and wind, many migrating birds make this island their first spring landfall as they make their way across the gulf from Mexico or Central America. But even if you don't come to watch neotropical birds fall from the sky (a breathtaking sight), there are still 164 acres of maritime pine forests, marshes and dunes to explore with winding trails to bird throughout. Over 400 bird species have been observed on Dauphin Island, including Swainson's warblers and black-whiskered vireos.

Runner-Up: Bon Secour National Wildlife Refuge

Alaska
Kenai Fjords National Park

Three hours south of Anchorage is Kenai Fjords National Park, where you can take specialized birding tours along the craggy coastline by boat, car or on foot. Nearly 200 species of birds have been documented in the park, including peregrine falcons, puffins (horned and tufted), black oyster-catchers and marbled murrelets. The park itself is set into the Kenai Peninsula. If you're in the area in May,

don't miss the Kenai Birding Festival. Novices and advanced birders will enjoy learning from bird experts, socializing with fellow enthusiasts and taking raft trips down the Kenai River to see how many species they can spot.

Runner-Up: Copper River Delta

Arizona
Chiricahua Mountains

You're guaranteed to see something unexpected when you visit the Chiricahua Mountains, host to 13 species of hummingbirds, some of which are rarely seen elsewhere north of Mexico. Don't forget to stop at the Chiricahua National Monument, towers of rhyolite rocks formed after a volcanic eruption millions of years ago. Many birds call this area home, including golden eagles and zone-tailed hawks. In the forested canyon bottoms, look for Arizona woodpecker and Grace's warbler.

Runners-Up: Ramsey Canyon Preserve and Sweetwater Wetlands

Arkansas
Ouachita National Forest

Cruise along Lake Ouachita on an organized bald eagle tour to observe the birds wintering in the area. Keep your eyes on the water, too, because many loons winter on the lake. Come back in July and August to see tens of thousands of purple martins roosting on Bird Island. There's plenty of bird wildlife to see away from the lake, too, including brown-headed nuthatch and red-cockaded woodpecker.

Runner-Up: Cache River National Wildlife Refuge

GRACE'S WARBLER

Chiricahua National Monument, Arizona

BROWN PELICAN

SWAINSON'S HAWK

California
Sonny Bono Salton Sea National Wildlife Refuge

Just north of El Centro, California, this wildlife refuge provides a habitat for wintering water birds like snow and Ross's geese, northern pintails, eared grebes and brown pelicans. It's the best place in the U.S. to find the yellow-footed gull, most numerous in late summer and fall. November through May are the best months for bird-watching at the Salton Sea, with heavy migrations of waterfowl, marsh and shorebirds during spring and fall. With more than 375 species of birds recorded, the Salton Sea has one of the most diverse ranges of species in the West.

Runner-Up: San Elijo Lagoon

Colorado
Pawnee National Grasslands

Transform your car into a bird blind when you take a self-guided tour through this short grass prairie that covers more than 193,000 acres. You'll be surprised by how many bird species you can spot from your car—the trick is to drive slowly, so you can see as many of the 301 species that have been observed here. (Visitors on foot are more likely to scare away prairie residents.) Among the birds you can expect to see are lark bunting, burrowing owl, mountain plover and horned lark. In late spring the grasslands are in full bloom. Make sure to check out Chalk Bluffs, a nesting site for ferruginous hawks, prairie falcons and Swainson's hawks.

Runner-Up: Arapaho National Wildlife Refuge

Connecticut
Coastal Center at Milford Point

Situated on an 8.4-acre barrier beach, this Audubon Society site has plenty of optimum bird-watching opportunities, including a 70-foot observation tower for a panoramic view. More than 300 species of birds have been observed at Milford Point, with the area's 840-acre saltwater marsh being an important stop for many migrating birds. Besides providing a variety of habitats such as coastal dunes and tide pools, the Coastal Center also is a teaching hub on the importance of preserving the ecosystem. You can get a taste of life at the Coastal Center without leaving home by going to *ctaudubon.org* to watch seasonal digital streaming of an osprey nest.

Runner-Up: White Memorial Conservation Center

OSPREY

Bombay Hook National Wildlife Refuge, Delaware

list, like American oystercatchers, marbled godwits, northern gannets, piping plovers and black skimmers. You'll find scoters and loons swimming offshore, and clapper rails and marsh wrens lurking in the salt marshes. When you're ready for a change of pace, take a guided walk around the island to look for nesting loggerhead sea turtles.

Runner-Up: Okefenokee National Wildlife Refuge

Delaware
Bombay Hook National Wildlife Refuge

Pace yourself; there's a lot to see at Delaware's most popular birding site, from hundreds of thousands of greater snow geese in the winter to songbirds in the spring. Open every day of the year from sunrise to sunset, the refuge spans nearly 16,000 acres and features five walking trails and three observation towers. A road loops around salt marshes, mudflats, woodlands and fields, so you can experience the wildlife from your vehicle. Stop by the Visitor Center to read the bird-sighting log and add a few of your own observations.

Runner-Up: White Clay Creek State Park

Florida
J.N. "Ding" Darling National Wildlife Refuge

This refuge gets its name from the editorial cartoonist and conservationist who founded the National Wildlife Federation. Home to more than 245 bird species, including roseate spoonbill, red-shouldered hawk and white ibis, this refuge protects endangered species and supplies roosting areas for migrating birds. There are plenty of trails to walk, and visitors can explore the refuge by bicycle. Volunteers track weekly bird observations online at *fws.gov/dingdarling*, and visiting birders can join in on the fun, too.

Runner-Up: Corkscrew Swamp Sanctuary

Georgia
Jekyll Island

Ten miles of tidal beaches means plenty of shorebirds, wading birds and waterfowl to add to your birding life

Hawaii
Waikamoi Preserve

There are only an estimated 500 kiwikiu or Maui parrotbills left in the world, and the best place to see them is at the Waikamoi Preserve, a 8,951-acre sanctuary on East Maui for threatened and endangered Hawaiian birds. Other native birds you might see include the crimson 'apapane and the yellow-green 'amakihi. Because of how delicate this habitat is, a guided hike led by an ornithologist from the National Park Service is the best way to experience everything the preserve has to offer, so plan ahead. It will be worth the effort for this once-in-a-lifetime experience.

Runner-Up: Hawaii Volcanoes National Park

ROSEATE SPOONBILL

AMERICAN OYSTERCATCHER

Jekyll Island, Georgia

BALD EAGLE

Idaho
Morley Nelson Snake River Birds of Prey National Conservation Area
If you're a raptor fan, this conservation area, which boasts the highest density of nesting raptors in North America, is a must-visit. Watch for bald eagles, ferruginous hawks, red-tailed hawks, golden eagles and American kestrels. Along the Snake River Canyon, 150 to 200 pairs of prairie falcons nest every year. But there aren't just raptors here—songbirds like lazuli bunting and Say's phoebe also nest in the riparian bottomlands.
Runner-Up: American Falls Reservoir

Illinois
Montrose Point Bird Sanctuary
Although this sanctuary is small, at about 15 acres, it has a lot to offer,

Montrose Point Bird Sanctuary, Illinois

SNOWY OWL

particularly during spring and fall migration when sparrows like white-crowned, Lincoln's and fox fill the meadow in the center of the sanctuary. Over 300 species of birds have been observed here, including extreme rarities such as reddish egret, Barrow's goldeneye and mottled duck. Come back during the winter months to see snowy owl, short-eared owl, snow bunting and Lapland longspur.
Runner-Up: Carlyle Lake

Indiana
Indiana Dunes State Park
Any one of this state park's trails through prairie, savanna, beach and dune habitats will net plenty of bird sightings, but the two best for birders are Trails 2 and 10. Take Trail 2 and enjoy a mile-long boardwalk where you can spot nesting woodland birds like hooded warbler, veery and red-shouldered hawk. Trail 10 runs along the high dunes and is a great spot to see pileated woodpeckers. Other birds that have been observed in the 2,182-acre park include little blue heron, harlequin duck and Kirtland's warbler. (Psst—check out the "3 Dune Challenge," if you're up for a serious hike.)
Runner-Up: Goose Pond Fish and Wildlife Area

Iowa
Cone Marsh State Wildlife Management Area
You'll have to leave your tent and camping gear at home when you visit this marshy area, because it's purposefully kept undisturbed. That's good news for bird enthusiasts, though, because the lack of human commotion makes for some choice bird-watching opportunities. Birds that have been spotted in this lowland area include rusty blackbirds, lark sparrows, black-crowned night-herons and swamp sparrows.
Runner-Up: Makoke Trail

Kansas
Cheyenne Bottoms
Smack-dab in the middle of the contiguous states, Cheyenne Bottoms is a primary migration route for

hundreds of bird species. This 41,000-acre wetland has a quarter of a million waterfowl and shorebirds that use it as a migration pit stop every year. Spring is the best time to visit, with wading birds like herons and sandhill cranes arriving in March and April, and shorebirds like dowitchers and lesser yellowlegs arriving in early May.
Runner-Up: Cimarron National Grassland

Indiana Dunes State Park, Indiana

PILEATED WOODPECKER

What to Pack
Don't worry about fitting a fancy spotting scope in your bag. Just make sure you have the essentials: a good pair of binoculars; a comprehensive field guide; a digital camera; and a journal to record your sightings.

DOWITCHER

Kentucky

John James Audubon State Park

It would be hard to find a birder who hasn't heard the name "Audubon." John James Audubon was a pioneer naturalist who wrote and illustrated *The Birds of America* over several decades in the 1800s. From 1810 to about 1819, he lived in Henderson, Kentucky, where this park and museum now display many of his original prints. Once you've experienced some birding history firsthand, take off on one of the nine hiking trails on the property, and see the birds and wildlife that helped to inspire one of America's finest ornithologists.

Runner-Up: Mammoth Cave National Park

Louisiana

Grand Isle

This barrier island is a Louisiana birding hot spot at any time of year, but a good month to visit Grand Isle is April during the Migratory Bird Celebration. This event includes activities like bird-watching tours, bird presentations, and even some bird-related games and prizes for kids. Walk through Grand Isle's oak-hackberry woods during spring migration and see how many species, like orioles, grosbeaks and buntings, you can spot.

Runner-Up: Peveto Woods Bird & Butterfly Sanctuary

ATLANTIC PUFFINS

Machias Seal Island, Maine

Maine

Machias Seal Island

Climb aboard a tour boat and take a trip across the Bay of Fundy to this 15-acre island and breeding colony. You'll see Atlantic puffin, razorbill, common murres and common and Arctic terns. Schedule your trip for the summer to see those species, but make sure to call well in advance to secure a visit. Island landings are limited due to its status as a designated sanctuary. But don't worry if you can't land—you'll still be able to see a lot from the boat.

Runner-Up: Acadia National Park

Maryland

Conowingo Dam

Whether you come for the bald eagles and stay for the gulls, or the other way around, there's a lot to see at Conowingo Dam. When December rolls around, the bald eagle population grows, and if you wait, you'll see them diving for fish. This is also a great time to watch for gulls, which can number in the thousands and often include a few rare species. Plus, don't miss the great blue herons that reside here all year long.

Runner-Up: Assateague Island National Seashore

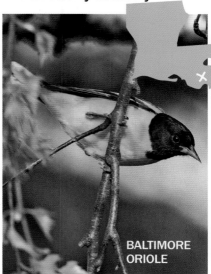

BALTIMORE ORIOLE

Conowingo Dam, Maryland

Massachusetts
Plum Island
Although this popular birding spot is an island, visitors can still get there by car thanks to a short bridge connecting it to the mainland. A classic spot to see snowy owls, the spring and fall seasons also attract a variety of waterfowl and songbirds. By late summer, the shorebird migration is in full swing.
Runner-Up: Sudbury Reservoir

WOOD DUCK

Michigan
Whitefish Point Bird Observatory
Located on Lake Superior in the Upper Peninsula, tens of thousands of migrating birds, like whimbrels, blue

GREAT HORNED OWL

jays, and sharp-shinned hawks, pass through this peninsula to reach their northern breeding grounds in spring or warmer winter homes in fall. And if you love owls, make sure to visit in April through mid-May, when species like boreal, great gray, great horned, short-eared and long-eared are passing through.
Runner-Up: Kellogg Bird Sanctuary

Minnesota
Sax-Zim Bog
If you're looking to shake off the winter doldrums, drive 50 miles northwest of Duluth to see boreal bird species, including black-backed woodpecker, boreal chickadee, and Connecticut warbler. The big draw for many birders, however, is the large great gray owl, which uses the bog as its wintering ground.
Runner-Up: Gunflint Trail

Mississippi
Sam D. Hamilton Noxubee National Wildlife Refuge
Short on time, but still want to cross a bird off your life list? Take the half-mile woodpecker trail at this 48,000-acre refuge, where you'll be able to spot many native woodpecker species, including the endangered red-cockaded woodpecker. Of course,

it's easy enough to spend the day, exploring the hiking trails and observing more birds like barred owl, northern bobwhite and wood ducks. (But watch out for the alligators.)
Runner-Up: Gulf Islands National Seashore

Missouri
Ted Shanks Conservation Area
Grab your favorite spotting scope and explore the diverse surroundings of this 6,705-acre area. Bottomland forests create excellent nesting habitats, and waterfowl are drawn to the many lakes and pools. Species that have been observed here include yellow-billed cuckoo, Mississippi kite, American tree sparrow and great blue heron. Go back in the evening for great night birding opportunities.
Runner-Up: Swan Lake National Wildlife Refuge

YELLOW-BILLED CUCKOO

Don't Break the Bank
Keep within your birding budget. Go camping instead of staying at a hotel, and use a guide from a local Audubon group instead of going on a costly bird tour.

Nebraska
Rowe Sanctuary

Thousands of sandhill cranes fill the skies of Nebraska every year, and one of the best spots to observe this heart-stirring spectacle is the Rowe Sanctuary. In March and early April, trained guides lead visitors out to strategically placed blinds to watch the cranes land along the Platte River. The sanctuary also hosts educational workshops, so visitors can learn even more about these fascinating birds.
Runner-Up: Fort Niobrara National Wildlife Refuge

Nevada
Ash Meadows National Wildlife Refuge

Don't be fooled by this refuge's desert location. Thanks to its many oases, including the largest in the Mojave Desert, this 28,000-acre refuge has wetlands and springs, making for some amazing biodiversity. One can't-miss bird-watching spot at the refuge is the Crystal Reservoir, where a clear shoreline offers views of western grebe and cinnamon teal. Look for Virginia rails and soras at Point of Rocks.
Runner-Up: Ruby Lake National Wildlife Refuge

New Hampshire
White Mountain National Forest

Songbirds like the American redstart and black-throated blue warbler spend their summers in this forest to build their nests and raise their young, so the best time to visit is in late spring and early summer. There are plenty of year-round residents to observe as well, like great horned owls, nuthatches and downy woodpeckers. When you want a bird-watching break, take a drive on the Kancamagus Highway for excellent views of the highest mountains in this part of the U.S.
Runner-Up: Odiorne Point State Park

White Mountain National Forest, New Hampshire

Montana
Glacier National Park

This one is a classic birding spot that's impossible to beat. The gorgeous mountain scenery is an excellent backdrop for the more than 260 species of birds that can be found here, like white-tailed ptarmigan, dusky grouse and chestnut-backed chickadee. A particularly good birding trail is the McDonald Creek Oxbow, where you'll find a diverse array of warbler species, plus harlequin ducks.
Runner-Up: Medicine Lake National Wildlife Refuge

DUSKY GROUSE

New Jersey
Cape May Bird Observatory

Swap your best bird stories with other birders at the Hawk Watch Platform in fall, while you observe the passage of migrating hawks, like sharp-shinned hawk, broad-winged hawk and peregrine falcon. The observatory also organizes the World Series of Birding, a 24-hour competition where the winning team has to spot the most bird species. *Birds & Blooms* sponsored the observatory's "birding by bike" team. Its final bird total was 126 species sighted this year.
Runner-Up: Sandy Hook

New Mexico
Bosque del Apache National Wildlife Refuge

This refuge is popular with wildlife photographers for a reason. No matter what season you visit this refuge along the Rio Grande, you won't be disappointed. Winter here means sandhill cranes, snow geese and Ross's goose. In summer, it's least bittern and occasionally white-faced ibis. Spring and fall are also excellent times to visit, thanks to hundreds of migrating bird species. It's impossible to see everything this refuge has to offer over the course of just one season, so plan to return often.
Runner-Up: Sandia Crest

New York
Jamaica Bay Wildlife Refuge

When you think of New York City, you probably don't picture acres of wetlands, but this refuge, nestled between Brooklyn and Queens, will surprise you. Over the last 25 years, more than 325 bird species have been observed here, including Eurasian wigeon, green-winged teal and northern pintail. One of the best birding spots is the East Pond, 100 acres of marsh used by thousands of shorebirds as a stopover during late summer and fall migrations.
Runner-Up: Adirondack Mountains

North Carolina
Pea Island National Wildlife Refuge

There's a good reason this 31,543-acre refuge was primarily established as a habitat for migrating birds. Hundreds of species stop here in spring and fall. Ospreys and bald eagles take advantage of the opportunities to nest near open water, while least tern and American oystercatchers reside along

EURASIAN WIGEON

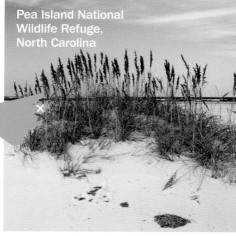

Pea Island National Wildlife Refuge, North Carolina

the refuge's ample beaches. There are plenty of trails for hiking, but if you're searching for a new perspective on the beauty of the Outer Banks, you can tour the area via kayak.
Runner-Up: Chimney Rock State Park

North Dakota
Lostwood National Wildlife Refuge

Glaciers from 10,000 years ago are responsible for this area's rolling hills and wetlands. One of the largest mixed grass prairies in the country, this refuge is home to more than 243 species, including sharp-tailed grouse, Sprague's pipit and grasshopper sparrow. Once thought to be extinct, giant Canada geese, a subspecies of Canada geese, have been reintroduced to the area and now nest here.
Runner-Up: J. Clark Salyer National Wildlife Refuge

Bosque del Apache National Wildlife Refuge, New Mexico

Magee Marsh
Wildlife Area, Ohio

Ohio
Magee Marsh Wildlife Area

This is one of those birding spots you're going to come back to year after year—and you won't be alone. Thousands of bird enthusiasts flock to this area for the Biggest Week in American Birding, a 10-day festival that celebrates everything birding and boasts hundreds of warblers. But even if you don't come for the festivities, there's plenty to enjoy, and the famous boardwalk is worth walking any time of the year.
Runner-Up: Killdeer Plains Wildlife Area

Oklahoma
Black Mesa State Park

About 30 million years ago, a layer of

SCALED QUAIL

black lava rock coated this mesa, which is where it gets its name. Today, there's no lack of bird species, like scaled quail, black-chinned hummingbirds, black-billed magpies, pinyon jays and many more. Once you've added a few birds to your life list, wait until dark for a special treat: every August, the Perseid meteor shower is visible in the night sky.
Runner-Up: Little River National Wildlife Refuge

Pennsylvania
Middle Creek Wildlife Management Area

Want to witness something truly spectacular? Visit Middle Creek in March to watch as hundreds of thousands of migrating snow geese, tundra swans and Canada geese come to roost on the 360-acre lake at dawn and dusk. When summer rolls around, look for bobolinks and other songbirds. There are plenty of trails

to explore, but if you want a touch more adventure, try one of the equestrian trails.
Runner-Up: Hawk Mountain Sanctuary

TUNDRA SWAN

BLACK-CROWNED NIGHT-HERON

Upper Klamath National Wildlife Refuge, Oregon

Oregon
Upper Klamath National Wildlife Refuge

This freshwater marsh is paradise for thousands of water birds, like American white pelican, black-crowned night-heron and black tern. Grab a paddle and make your way down the 9.5-mile canoe run that winds through the marsh. This is a great way to see even more bird species, including Virginia rail, Clark's grebes and sora.
Runner-Up: Coos Bay

LEAST TERN

Huntington Beach
State Park, South Carolina

Rhode Island

**Trustom Pond National
Wildlife Refuge**

It will be hard to walk away from this refuge without becoming more of a bird expert, thanks to the knowledgeable volunteer staff at the visitor station, plus the detailed interpretive panels scattered throughout the two miles of nature trails and four viewing platforms. As the only undeveloped coastal salt pond in Rhode Island, this refuge is an important habitat for 300 bird species, like least tern and piping plover, which use the barrier beach as a nesting site.
**Runner-Up: Sachuest Point National
Wildlife Refuge**

South Carolina

Huntington Beach State Park

If you're going to hit one birding spot in South Carolina, make it this one. Winter is the best time to explore this park, when you're most likely to see resident bald eagles and various waterfowl, like gadwall and green-winged teal. Walk over to the jetty to observe black skimmers and royal tern. If you look really close, you might be able to see camouflaged purple sandpipers as well.
**Runner-Up: Savannah
National Wildlife Refuge**

South Dakota

Black Hills National Forest

There's so much to see in the Black Hills of western South Dakota, but a few highlights include the ponderosa pine forests, where pine siskin, red crossbill and red-breasted nuthatch reside. Walk further up the mountains where white spruce forests become more common, and you'll find three-toed woodpeckers, brown creepers and golden-crowned kinglets. Oh, there is also that little attraction known as Mount Rushmore.
**Runner-Up: Sand Lake National
Wildlife Refuge**

A Big Year

Thinking of doing a big year? Before you set off on a birding quest, decide what type of big year you want. Do you want to see as many bird species as you can, or do you want to have a specific goal, like focusing on species on your life list? Are you going to limit yourself to your state or travel further? Planning ahead is key!

GOLDEN-CROWNED KINGLET

Black Hills,
South Dakota

Great Smoky Mountains
National Park, Tennessee

Tennessee
Great Smoky Mountains National Park

A day of birding in this popular national park is going to be a very rewarding one: If you know most birds by sight and sound, you'll easily see 100 species a day during peak migration in late April and early May. There's a dizzying amount of habitat diversity here. Southern hardwoods at low elevations have yellow-billed cuckoos, Louisiana waterthrushes and black-and-white warblers, while open fields have red-tailed hawks, killdeer and yellow warblers. And that's just a start!
Runner-Up: Reelfoot National Wildlife Refuge

Texas
Rio Grande Valley

Everything is bigger in Texas, and that includes birding. The Rio Grande Valley is home to nine unique bird-centric locations, like the Bentsen-Rio Grande Valley State Park where you'll be able to spot plenty of kiskadees, green kingfishers and plain chachalacas, and the Roma Bluffs, which are home to red-billed pigeon and brown jay. Don't miss the Rio Grande Valley Birding Festival in early November.
Runner-Up: Guadalupe Mountains National Park

Utah
Antelope Island State Park

Although this park is most known for its bison herd, there's plenty here for bird nerds, like huge populations of black-necked stilts, white-faced ibis and California gulls that nest along the Great Salt Lake. The island itself has a lot of grassland habitat for burrowing owls, chukars and long-billed curlews.
Runner-Up: Ouray National Wildlife Refuge

GREEN KINGFISHER

Antelope Island State Park, Utah

CALIFORNIA GULL

GRASSHOPPER SPARROW

Vermont
Dead Creek Wildlife Management Area

Despite its name, this wildlife area is incredibly lively, with over 200 species of birds and 3,000 acres of deciduous forests, fields and wetlands. It also boasts a surprising number of state endangered species, like grasshopper sparrows and upland sandpipers. But even if you don't catch a glimpse of these birds, there's still plenty to see, including enormous flocks of Canada geese and snow geese. They use this area as a stopover during migration.
Runner-Up: Missisquoi National Wildlife Refuge

Virginia
Kiptopeke State Park

If you've ever wanted to see bird banding up close, this is the place. Songbirds have been banded at this station since the early 1960s, and a raptor banding station has since been added. From September through

Kiptopeke State Park, Virginia

November, volunteers record the number of hawks that fly overhead. (Since the program started, they've counted nearly 750,000 hawks!)
Runner-Up: Chincoteague National Wildlife Refuge

Washington
Olympic National Park

As far as gorgeous backdrops go, it's hard to beat the lush rain forests and breathtaking mountaintops of Olympic National Park. It's also hard to beat the diverse number of bird species the park has to offer at more than 250. Woodpeckers, blue grouse and gray jays can be found in the mountain meadows, while rhinoceros auklets and western gulls nest along the coast. To cover more ground, take the Olympic Loop, a self-guided driving tour of the park.
Runner-Up: Grays Harbor

Stamp Happy
Get a free year of admission to wildlife refuges by buying a Federal Duck Stamp at your local post office.

Olympic National Park, Washington

GREAT BLUE HERON

Horicon Marsh, Wisconsin

GREAT EGRETS

West Virginia

Green Bottom Wildlife Management Area

No matter what time of year you visit this 1,096-acre habitat, you will find multiple bird species. Located on a former plantation along the banks of the Ohio River, this wildlife area attracts more than 100 species of birds, including wood ducks, bald eagles and great blue herons. Nesting boxes and 14 man-made nesting islands encourage more birds to make themselves at home.

Runner-Up: Cranesville Swamp Natural Area

Wisconsin

Horicon Marsh

There's always something going on at the Horicon Marsh, the largest cattail marsh in the United States at over 33,000 acres. More than 300 birds have been spotted in this internationally recognized wetland, though this ecosystem is best known as a stopover for Canada geese. If you'd really like to dive in, visit during the annual Horicon Marsh Bird Festival in May and take part in boat tours, demonstrations of bird banding, night sound hikes and more.

Runner-Up: Crex Meadows Wildlife Area

Wyoming

Grand Teton National Park

Just south of Yellowstone, the 300 bird species that have been sighted here are as extreme as the landscape. You can spot both the smallest bird in North America, the calliope hummingbird, and the largest waterfowl, the trumpeter swan, in this park. With more than 200 miles of trails to explore, you'll never run out of options. Other notable species that have been spotted here include three-toed woodpecker, great gray owl, osprey and Brewer's sparrow.

Runner-Up: Edness K. Wilkins State Park

Grand Teton National Park, Wyoming

Birding in Canada

Look to our northern neighbor for even more excellent birding spots.

Cape Breton Highlands National Park, Nova Scotia, is a great spot for northern species like spruce grouse, boreal chickadee and pine grosbeak.

Point Pelee National Park, Ontario, is a migratory stop for nearly 200 species.

Visit **Kejimkujik National Park,** Nova Scotia, in the spring for northern parula and common loon.

Canada's Bird-Watching Hot Spots

The provinces and territories have amazing avian habitats.

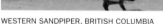

WESTERN SANDPIPER, BRITISH COLUMBIA

YELLOW WARBLER, POINT PELEE NATIONAL PARK

BLACK GUILLEMOTS, NOVA SCOTIA

1. GEORGE C. REIFEL MIGRATORY BIRD SANCTUARY

Delta, British Columbia

Highlights of this area include up to a million western sandpipers in spring and fall and wintering lesser snow geese that arrive in early October. The sanctuary offers several walkways, trails and "bird blinds" for prime bird viewing.

2. BEAVERHILL LAKE HERITAGE RANGELAND

Edmonton, Alberta

Recognized for its wetlands and as a Canadian Important Bird Area, Beaverhill Lake boasts diverse bird populations. About 145 bird species have been known to breed there. If you're nearby, stop at Beaverhill Bird Observatory for special bird-related events.

3. RIDING MOUNTAIN NATIONAL PARK

Wasagaming, Manitoba

Several habitats make up this park— boreal and hardwood forests and prairie grasslands. Expect to see great gray owls and spruce grouse. It's a year-round park, but summer is a great time to see lots of Connecticut warblers.

4. POINT PELEE NATIONAL PARK

Leamington, Ontario

Called "The Warbler Capital of Canada," 42 of 52 warbler species have been recorded here. This park is an important migration stop for many songbirds and hawks in both spring and fall. It draws about 300,000 visitors each year.

5. BIRD ISLAND IMPORTANT BIRD AREA

Cape Breton, Nova Scotia

Bird Island, actually two islands, offers great views of nesting birds such as great cormorants, Atlantic puffins, razorbills and black guillemots. Book a boat tour to head to the islands to see these awesome breeding birds.

Provincial Birds of Canada

Alberta – Great horned owl
British Columbia – Steller's jay
Manitoba – Great gray owl
New Brunswick – Black-capped chickadee
Newfoundland & Labrador – Atlantic puffin

Nova Scotia – Osprey
Ontario – Common loon
Prince Edward Island – Blue jay
Quebec – Snowy owl
Saskatchewan – Sharp-tailed grouse

Did You Know? Canada doesn't have a national bird. What do you think it should be?

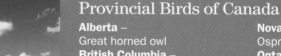

Birding the National Parks

Fantastic sightings are nearly guaranteed when you plan your trip around these magnificent destinations.

BY KEN KEFFER

Since the establishment of Yellowstone National Park in 1872, the federal government has preserved some of the continent's most spectacular scenery for the enjoyment of all. With this amazing backdrop of unique habitats, it's not surprising that national parks are also top birding destinations. Let's explore some of the best of the best.

Heron at Everglades
National Park

Big Bend National Park, TEXAS

With more than 450 documented bird species, Big Bend has recorded more than any other national park. This generous expanse of west Texas covers a wide range of habitats from the banks of the Rio Grande to the rugged Chisos Mountains.

The Colima warbler is more common in Mexico, but a few can be found in the mountains of Big Bend. Other Southwestern species include the hepatic tanager, painted redstart, Scott's oriole and Mexican jay. Big Bend is also a good place to look for hummingbirds, including the rare Lucifer hummingbird, found more regularly here than anywhere else in the U.S.

Big Bend National Park

Colima warbler in Big Bend

Clark's nutcracker in Grand Teton National Park

Yellowstone & Grand Teton National Parks, WYOMING

As a Wyoming native, I've always had great pride in Yellowstone and neighboring Grand Teton. When I hear the hoarse squawks of the Clark's nutcracker, I imagine what it was like for the early explorers of the area.

You'll spot other creatures with the birds. A couple of my favorite viewing spots are Fishing Bridge and Two Ocean Lake. From the bridge, watch for American white pelicans, river otters, or maybe even a grizzly bear looking to make a snack out of the native cutthroat trout. Another big white bird on the waters of northwest Wyoming is the trumpeter swan, often nesting on Two Ocean Lake. In winter, the swan population grows as migratory birds join the individuals that remain in the region year-round. Fires are an important part of the Yellowstone ecosystem, and I'm always excited to spot woodpeckers and colorful fireweed in areas that were once burned over.

Hikers in Grand Teton National Park

PREVIOUS SPREAD: BRIAN LASENBY/SHUTTERSTOCK.COM; KATHY ADAMS CLARK/KAC PRODUCTIONS; GREG LASLEY/KAC PRODUCTIONS (WARBLER). THIS SPREAD: STEVE AND DAVE MASLOWSKI

Roseate spoonbills
in Everglades National Park

Blackburnian warbler in Great
Smoky Mountains National Park

Great Smoky Mountains
National Park

Everglades National Park, FLORIDA

In this vast wetland, mangrove thickets rim freshwater saw grass prairies, which open out into the salty Atlantic Ocean and Gulf of Mexico. It's a park best viewed from the water, even if all you have time for is an afternoon paddle. Hiking trails and boardwalks also allow visitors to get prime views of the many species of wading birds.

Look for flocks of white ibis foraging in the shallow waters, their long bills probing the mud. You can also find rare wood storks balancing awkwardly in treetops. Roseate spoonbills look unworldly with their pink feathers and spatulate bills. Anhingas sit drying their wings on nearly every available perch. Visitors can also expect to find alligators sunning themselves at water's edge, so watch where you step.

Great Smoky Mountains National Park, TENNESSEE AND NORTH CAROLINA

Tucked along the mountains, Great Smoky has more human visitors than any other national park in America. It's also a popular place for birds and critters. For plants, this is one of the most diverse places on the continent, boasting 100 native tree species and 1,500 kinds of flowering plants.

The park is at a crossroads for birds. Southern species can be spotted in the lowlands, while birds more common in the North inhabit the higher elevations. For example, both Carolina and black-capped chickadees live here. Other Southern highlights include yellow-throated vireos,

Support and Save
You can pay $80 to get an annual pass to all federal recreation sites. Learn more at *nps.gov/findapark/passes.htm.*

hooded warblers and Louisiana waterthrush, while Northern birds rare in other parts of the South include golden-crowned kinglets, veery, winter wren, northern saw-whet owls, and black-throated blue, Blackburnian, chestnut-sided and Canada warblers.

Acadia National Park, MAINE

This expanse of coastal Maine was the country's first Eastern national park. Whether by car, carriage, bus, bike or boat, it's worth exploring fully. The scenic vistas of the rugged North Atlantic are impressive enough, but the backdrop of Acadia includes Cadillac Mountain, the highest point on the East Coast.

Nearly two dozen species of warbler have nested in Acadia. Peregrine falcons nest along the cliffs of Precipice Trail, and this is also a noted raptor migration site. Waterfowl include scoters, eiders and guillemots, which congregate during the winter. Be sure to check out the Wild Gardens of Acadia, too, where the diverse plant life can be really active with birds.

Point Pelee National Park, ONTARIO

One of the smallest national parks in Ontario, Point Pelee, at the southernmost tip of Canada, is of critical importance to birds. A peninsula jutting into Lake Erie, it's like an airport landing strip for many migrating species.

An impressive array of shorebirds, warblers and thrushes move through the park each year. You can also see scarlet tanagers, blue jays and both Baltimore and orchard orioles in good numbers during migration. The area is host to great movements of raptors, too. Some species, like northern harriers, osprey and peregrine falcons, will eventually fly across Lake Erie, but broad-winged, red-tailed and red-shouldered hawks tend to avoid flying over open water. They will generally follow the coast along the western shores of Lake Erie on their southern migration.

With 59 national parks in the U.S. and almost as many in Canada, you could argue that every one of them is a worthy birding destination. So get out there and explore them. You'll be rewarded with gorgeous scenery, unique habitats and some of the best birding around.

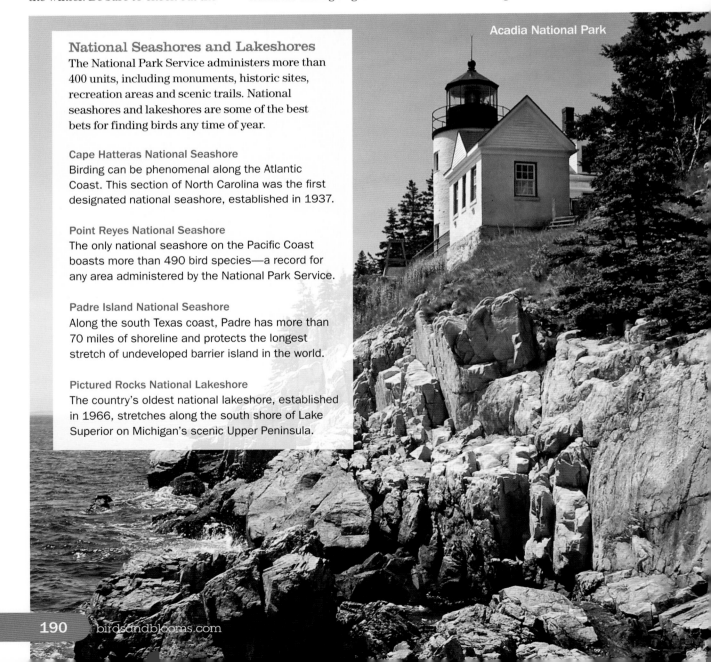

Acadia National Park

National Seashores and Lakeshores
The National Park Service administers more than 400 units, including monuments, historic sites, recreation areas and scenic trails. National seashores and lakeshores are some of the best bets for finding birds any time of year.

Cape Hatteras National Seashore
Birding can be phenomenal along the Atlantic Coast. This section of North Carolina was the first designated national seashore, established in 1937.

Point Reyes National Seashore
The only national seashore on the Pacific Coast boasts more than 490 bird species—a record for any area administered by the National Park Service.

Padre Island National Seashore
Along the south Texas coast, Padre has more than 70 miles of shoreline and protects the longest stretch of undeveloped barrier island in the world.

Pictured Rocks National Lakeshore
The country's oldest national lakeshore, established in 1966, stretches along the south shore of Lake Superior on Michigan's scenic Upper Peninsula.

The Kaufman Top 5

Kenn and Kimberly Kaufman, our bird experts, list their favorite birding spots in the U.S.

Morro Bay, California

Great kiskadee, South Texas

Egrets in the Florida Keys

1. MORRO BAY, CALIFORNIA

This globally important bird area hosts an impressive number of wintering birds including marbled godwit and willet, along with breathtaking coastline scenery.

Kim's best memory: Getting her lifer, Heermann's gull, which she describes as "a handsome, elegant bird."

2. PATAGONIA LAKE, ARIZONA

This is the best spot in the U.S. to see elegant trogon and various flycatchers in winter. A boat ride or hike along the lake provides a wide variety of birds amid alluring landscapes.

Kim's best memory: Seeing violet-green swallows, a western swallow similar to tree swallows.

3. RIO GRANDE VALLEY, SOUTH TEXAS

Birders of every level will love the colorful kiskadees, noisy chachalacas and boisterous green jays amid desert, forest, grassland and tropical ecosystems. You can find about 50 native birds exclusive to this location.

Kenn's best memory: Meeting Kim while leading a birding trip and afterwards, bonding over an olive sparrow.

4. MAGEE MARSH, OHIO

The Kaufmans live near this iconic hot spot on the Lake Erie shoreline where hundreds of colorful warblers and other songbird migrants can be seen at eye level nearly every day in May.

Kim's best memory: When Kenn tweeted that he'd discovered the federally endangered Kirtland's warbler here—and hundreds came to see it.

5. FLORIDA KEYS

Large wading birds, including herons, ibis and spoonbills grace the coastline and backwaters in a relaxed setting, and there's always a chance for a rarity. Meandering through mangrove swamps and hammock woods in winter will give you plenty of warbler and other songbird views.

Kenn's best memory: Finding the rare western spindalis, formerly called stripe-headed tanager, when he was 18.

Bufflehead

Home is Where the Birds Are

Kenn and Kimberly say their No. 1 birding spot is their own backyard. They've documented 126 species in two years on two acres of restored prairie, a pond and a creek adjacent to farm fields. They recently added bufflehead to their yard list, and have been planting native vegetation, like sawtooth sunflowers, to attract birds.

10 Bird-Friendly Cities

These communities fly high when it comes to preserving and protecting urban habitat.

Chicago skyline

With 80 percent of Americans living in cities, thank goodness birding isn't limited to rural areas. Hundreds of cities across the country are bustling with bird activity and taking steps to keep it that way. The proof is in the success of programs like the National Wildlife Federation's Community Wildlife Habitat certification and the National Audubon Society's Lights Out campaign. You can also see it in the thousands of birders who rally like-minded individuals to make their communities better—and safer—for winged activity.

This list of 10 outstanding cities considers a number of factors, including bird-friendly ordinances and programs, habitat creation and preservation efforts, and birding activities and events. Yet it only skims the surface of the many fantastic birding opportunities in cities from coast to coast. Use our list as a guide, but also let it inspire you to go out and explore in a city near you!

BY HEATHER LAMB

Chicago, Illinois

This city's success proves that urban life and wildlife can coexist. Among other achievements, it was the first U.S. city to launch a Lights Out campaign. (Toronto spearheaded a similar initiative in Canada.) This partnership with the Audubon Society encourages building owners to darken unneeded lights at night during migration periods to prevent birds from becoming disoriented. It's estimated that it saves more than 10,000 warblers, thrushes and other migratory birds every year.

Tucson, Arizona

With a desert climate, mountains on all sides and seasonal monsoons, Tucson is full of unique species like Gambel's quail, cactus wrens and rare hummingbirds—and a dedicated birding community aims to preserve those attributes. The Tucson Audubon Society sponsors an urban program that supports bird-friendly landscapes, and locals have taken part in the annual Tucson Bird Count since 2001.

Gambel's quail

Fayetteville, Arkansas

Home to the University of Arkansas, this Ozark Mountains city teems with opportunities to see birds, including a network of birding trails, many along former railways, and 200-acre Lake Fayetteville supports a myriad of species. Trails through the 450 acres surrounding the lake intersect varied habitats, including open water, woodlands and grasslands, and provide easy access for spotting buffleheads, warblers, vireos and others.

Red-eyed vireo

Aurora, Colorado

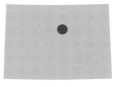

Domestic cats kill at least 1.3 billion birds a year, according to a 2012 federally sponsored study, so it's not surprising that some cities have put restrictions on free-roaming felines. One of those communities is Aurora, a Denver suburb whose 20-year-old ordinance limits the number of cats per household, among other provisions. The city is also rich with publicly accessible bird habitats, including prairie at Cherry Creek State Park, and the Quincy Reservoir, which gives residents and visitors a chance to see birds like Swainson's hawks.

Swainson's hawk

Fort Lauderdale, Florida

This was one of the first places certified as a National Wildlife Federation Community Wildlife Habitat. With the Atlantic Ocean to the east and the Everglades to the west, it's a mecca for many resident and migrating species. Waterbirds thrive along the city's shoreline. In 2013, a section of beach was roped off to protect the nests of about 100 least terns, a threatened species whose appearance delighted locals.

Least tern

Wood thrush

Takoma Park, Maryland

North of Washington, D.C., Takoma Park is known for its progressive policies. In 2013, this community of 17,000 became the first municipality of its size to ban the use of lawn pesticides for cosmetic purposes on both public and private land. The movement began as a leaflet campaign spearheaded by two neighbors and three years later passed unanimously. But that isn't all this community has going for birds. Sligo Creek bisects the city and provides habitat for species like wood thrushes and yellow-crowned night-herons.

Sanderlings

Cape May, New Jersey

Situated between the Atlantic Ocean and Delaware Bay, the Cape May peninsula and this city at its southern tip are a paradise for migrating birds traveling along the Atlantic flyway. The area's plentiful wetlands attract migrants like red knots, ruddy turnstones, semipalmated sandpipers and sanderlings. It's a magnet for warblers as well, including the namesake Cape May warbler. Numerous protected areas, including South Cape May Meadows Preserve, offer habitat for hundreds of species.

Harlingen, Texas

This city just north of Mexico and west of the Gulf hosts one of the country's oldest birding celebrations. For over two decades, the Rio Grande Valley Birding Festival has drawn visitors from all over the world to see unique species like green jays and Altamira orioles. The success of the festival and the city are intertwined, with each supporting the other's growth, and the event's emphasis on ecotourism benefits nearby hot spots, including Laguna Atascosa and Santa Ana National Wildlife Refuges.

Green jays

Seattle, Washington

Surrounded by protected national forests and parks, Seattle aims to make its cityscapes safer for birds, too. One such endeavor is Seattle City Light's Avian Protection Program, which seeks to avert dangerous run-ins with electric utilities. Some adaptations include barriers around power lines and new nesting platforms along the Duwamish River, where osprey arrive in spring to fish for salmon and nest on the poles.

Osprey

Green Bay, Wisconsin

Located at the base of Wisconsin's "thumb," this football-famous city was one of the 15 inaugural communities in the Bird City Wisconsin program. This statewide initiative encourages communities to create habitats, protect birds and provide public education on avian conservation, and has named 91 Bird Cities so far. Among Green Bay's efforts are an active chimney swift monitoring program and a collaboration with Tree City USA to plant bird-friendly native trees.

Chimney swifts

When the city becomes the backyard

The National Wildlife Federation's Community Wildlife Habitat program recognizes the power of habitat creation that extends beyond the backyard and encourages communities to become involved. In 1998, Alpine, California, was the first community recognized, and about 78 have now been certified.

These cities, towns and villages must show a deep commitment to wildlife protection, creating and maintaining habitats in private yards and public spaces. The bigger the city, the more wildlife habitat it must maintain. Austin, Texas, has the most certified wildlife habitats in the country. The communities come

in all sizes. Chamblee, Georgia, a community of 9,800 near Atlanta, earned certification in 2003, while Baltimore, Charlotte and Chicago are still pursuing certification.

For more information, or to see a list of certified communities in your state, visit the Garden for Wildlife section of *nwf.org*.

the "birdiest" botanical gardens

Feathered beauty nests among the plants in bird-friendly spaces around the country.

BY SHERYL DEVORE

Tohono Chul Park

Botanical gardens are most known for their beautifully landscaped grounds and lavishly themed gardens. But did you know they are also superb places to watch birds? These gardens provide green space and water where birds can rest, feed, bathe and drink. To make these public places even more attractive to birds and bird-watchers, garden staff and volunteers are creating native gardens, erecting nesting boxes, leading nature walks and teaching classes on gardening for birds. Here are a few places where you can indulge a dual love of botanical and avian treasures together.

ARIZONA

★ Desert Botanical

★ Tohono

Desert Botanical Garden

Anna's hummingbird feeding on a cacti bloom at Desert Botanical Garden.

Desert Favorites

Tohono Chul Park lies within the Sonoran Desert in Tucson, Arizona. This park provides easy walking trails and vibrant botanical gardens to view some of the 140 bird species that visit the 49-acre site. A hummingbird garden attracts Costa's and Anna's hummingbirds year-round to sip nectar from salvia, desert willow and other plants. The Wildlife Garden features saguaro cacti where Gila woodpeckers build nests in spring.

The **Desert Botanical Garden** in Phoenix, Arizona, features a Desert Wildflower Loop Trail where you can view exhibits on wildflowers while watching hummingbirds. Greater roadrunners nest in candelabra cacti in the Ottosen Entry Garden. Bird lovers will especially enjoy the guided bird walks, which are held nearly every Monday at the 140-acre site.

TRAVEL TIP

Before visiting any botanical gardens, look online to learn which birds you can see and to download checklists, maps and other educational tools.

West Coast Gardens

Established as a teaching, living plant museum, the **University of California Riverside Botanic Gardens** has recorded 200 bird species within four miles of trails winding through native riparian habitats and exotic gardens. In spring, hooded orioles visit the maroon blossoms of the honeybush in the South African garden. The online UCR Avian Project offers photos and details of bird species at the garden, located on the university campus.

Mendocino Coast Botanical Gardens in Fort Bragg, California, has attracted more than 150 species of birds to its 47 acres of coastal, marine and inland habitats. The Mendocino Coast Audubon Society leads early bird and beginning bird walks year-round.

California quail

Mendocino
★ Coast

CALIFORNIA

UC Riverside
Botanic Gardens
★

Urban Gems

Smithsonian Gardens Urban Bird Habitat in Washington, D.C., invites visitors to learn about birds that live in cities. Garden staff recently repurposed a dying lacebark pine tree into a nesting, foraging and roosting spot for birds like woodpeckers. Native prairie flowers provide seeds to hungry finches and other seedeaters. Signs offer information on avian ecology and ways to create backyard habitats for birds.

Avondale Park Rose and Habitat Garden is getting a little help from a program called the Urban Bird Habitat Initiative. This space in Birmingham, Alabama, is being upgraded with 84 planting beds to attract birds. Volunteers also have installed a prairie garden in the Birmingham Museum of Art Prairie Habitat, where birds feast on plant seeds.

American goldfinch on purple coneflower

★ Avondale Park

ALABAMA

PLANTS FOR THE BIRDS

When visiting botanical gardens, take note of the plants. If you live nearby, you can use those plants in your own yard. Here are suggestions from the Smithsonian Gardens Urban Bird Habitat:

- Blackhaw viburnum
- Wax myrtle
- Spicebush
- Purple coneflower
- Sunflower

Gardens for Migrants

Chicago Botanic Garden in Glencoe, Illinois, attracts waves of migrants, including sparrows and warblers in spring and fall. Key spots in the 385-acre garden include McDonald Woods, the Sensory Garden, the Picnic Glen and the Waterfall Garden. In winter, visit feeders at the Buehler Enabling Garden to observe pine siskins, common redpolls and other hardy birds.

Longwood Gardens in Kennett Square, Pennsylvania, hosts birding tours year-round focusing on migrants, like ring-necked ducks and Northern pintails, that stop by the wetlands in March, and warblers that pass through in April and May.

Blackburnian warbler

PENNSYLVANIA

Longwood Gardens ★

Chicago Botanic Garden ★

ILLINOIS

You can see a waterfall and garden at Chicago Botanic Garden.

The Fairchild Tropical Botanic Garden has a special bird walk.

Eastern bluebird

★ Huntsville Garden

ALABAMA

FLORIDA

Fairchild Garden ★

Fairchild Tropical Botanic Garden in Coral Gables, Florida, features the James A. Kushlan Bird Walk, named after an ornithologist who leads a bird conservation program there. Go online to see a map of the two walking loops and which birds you're likely to find at various stops. For example, the map shows two places where you can find the common hill myna, native to southeastern Asia, but now established in Florida. Try the annual bird festival in October, where you can join bird walks for adults and children.

Best Birding Trails

Huntsville Botanical Gardens' Lewis Birding Trail in Huntsville, Alabama, meanders past Little Smith Lake, an active purple martin colony, a bluebird trail and feeder stations. The purple martins return each spring and can be seen flying in and out of man-made nest boxes and feeding their noisy young. A local birder created the trail for visitors to learn more about the birds that inhabit the garden.

Missouri Botanical Gardens

GARDEN GEMS
of the U.S.

Add these impressive public gardens to your travel bucket list.

BY PETER SETTER

Longwood Gardens

Denver Botanic Gardens

Plant and flower lovers should try to visit these luscious sanctuaries. Make one your destination, or add it to the end of a planned trip. Whether nestled in a lush forest or smack-dab in the middle of a metropolis, any one of these grand outdoor conservatories is worth the detour.

Missouri Botanical Garden
ST. LOUIS, MISSOURI

This 79-acre National Historic Landmark is one of the oldest botanical gardens in the U.S. The expansive grounds include a 14-acre Japanese garden featuring culturally influenced architecture and plantings, including lotuses, cherry blossoms, azaleas and chrysanthemums. The grounds also include 23 residential-scale demonstration gardens, founder Henry Shaw's 1849 country home, Tower Grove House, and one of the world's largest collections of rare and endangered orchids.

Longwood Gardens
KENNETT SQUARE, PENNSYLVANIA

Greater Philadelphia calls itself America's Garden Capital. One of more than 30 public gardens in the area, Longwood boasts more than a million visitors each year and has more than 1,000 acres of gardens, woodlands and meadows. You'll find special outdoor displays year-round, or you can venture into the country's largest conservatory, with 4.5 acres of indoor gardens.

Perhaps the most famous part of the gardens is the Main Fountain

Garden, featuring magnificent European-inspired Italian limestone fountains that shoot jets of water 130 feet into the air.

Denver Botanic Gardens
DENVER, COLORADO

The Denver Botanic Gardens' mission is to connect people with the plants of the Rocky Mountain region and similar regions around the world. The gardens are spread among three locations, but the main site is just 10 minutes east of downtown.

In addition to housing flora, the grounds also have indoor and outdoor

art exhibits, with landscape paintings, sculptures and photos. The renowned Rock Alpine Garden—one of about 45 individual gardens—has over 500 tons of rock and 2,300 species of plants.

Lewis Ginter Botanical Garden
RICHMOND, VIRGINIA

A healthy dose of Southern charm is injected throughout all 50 acres at Lewis Ginter. The Conservatory, crowned by a 63-foot-tall dome, is often called the "jewel of the garden." Inside, you can find exotic plants such as orchids, as well as seasonal themed

Lewis Ginter Botanical Garden

Desert Botanical Garden

displays. The Central Garden unites the grounds and features a variety of "rooms," such as the Healing and Fountain gardens.

Another highlight of Lewis Ginter is its interactive children's area, complete with a giant, accessible tree house.

Desert Botanical Garden
PHOENIX, ARIZONA

Founded in the 1930s by a group of volunteers who wanted to preserve the local flora, the Desert Botanical Garden is still run by more than 1,000 volunteers today. The 140-acre garden focuses solely on desert plants, and you can find 50,000 of them showcased in beautiful outdoor exhibits that dispel any expectations of a colorless desert landscape. The collection of cacti is unique, and several loop trails wander through an array of arid-adapted plants from the Sonoran Desert. A popular time to visit is spring, when the garden hosts its annual butterfly exhibit and wildflowers begin to bloom.

New York Botanical Garden
NEW YORK, NEW YORK

This 250-acre picturesque paradise, open year-round, is in the heart of Bronx, New York, and features an astonishing 50 gardens and more than a million plants.

Fifty acres of old-growth forest lie at the heart of the garden, the largest remnant of the original forest that covered all of New York City until the 17th century. If you're looking for a colorful show, be sure to visit in April or early May, when 25,000 tulips bloom.

New York Botanical Garden

5 AMAZING B&B GARDENS
If you're looking for a quick weekend getaway, consider these bed-and-breakfasts known for their accompanying gardens.

Black Walnut Point Inn
TILGHMAN, MARYLAND
Head to this private island estate to bask in 6 acres of landscaped gardens and lawns, then watch the sun set over Chesapeake Bay.

Pennsbury Inn
CHADDS FORD, PENNSYLVANIA
This certified wildlife habitat has acres of wooded gardens. Be sure to check out the herb garden for basil, thyme and oregano.

Pine River Ranch
LEAVENWORTH, WASHINGTON
At this quiet retreat on 22 acres of countryside, guests will be dazzled by the many colors and textures in the garden. Visit late in the season to see 10-foot-tall sunflowers.

Azalea Inn & Gardens
SAVANNAH, GEORGIA
This B&B boasts resilient native plants from the 19th century amid a private garden setting. You'll find plenty of its namesake flowers.

Vintage Towers Bed & Breakfast Inn
CLOVERDALE, CALIFORNIA
The showstoppers at this Queen Anne Victorian mansion are a 40-foot wisteria-covered veranda and a rose-covered wrought iron pavilion.

Stop and Smell the Roses

Soak in the radiance of these iconic blooms at popular public gardens.

Mesa Community College Rose Garden

Tyler Municipal Rose Garden

Elizabeth Park Heritage Rose Garden

1. WASHINGTON PARK'S INTERNATIONAL ROSE TEST GARDEN

Portland, Oregon

One of six testing sites for the American Rose Society's miniature roses, this garden also tests many other rose varieties for beauty, durability and growing ease. Free tours are held daily from Memorial Day weekend to Labor Day weekend. *portlandoregon .gov/parks*

2. MESA COMMUNITY COLLEGE ROSE GARDEN

Mesa, Arizona

Take a self-guided tour and enjoy this garden's 9,000 rose bushes. The Veteran's Rose Garden section alone has more than 60 rose varieties and every rose bed has a phone number you can call for more information about each one. *rosegarden.mesa cc.edu*

3. TYLER MUNICIPAL ROSE GARDEN

Tyler, Texas

This city is called the rose capital of the world for a reason: Its large rose garden boasts over 40,000 flowers. Every October, the garden has its annual Texas Rose Festival. Watch a parade of floats made with roses and tour fields, nurseries and municipal gardens with roses in full bloom. *visittyler.com/ tylerrosegarden*

4. GARDENS OF THE AMERICAN ROSE CENTER

Shreveport, Louisiana

At the national headquarters of the American Rose Society, you'll find more than 65 individual rose gardens across 118 acres, including a memorial prayer garden, fountains and sculptures. Look online for upcoming public events held at the center. *rose.org/our-gardens*

5. ELIZABETH PARK HERITAGE ROSE GARDEN

West Hartford, Connecticut

Step back in time at the Heritage Rose Garden, where you can explore arrays of old rose varieties, some of which date to 1867. Head back to the park's main garden to check out modern-day specialties like climbers and David Austin roses. *elizabethparkct.org*

Tournament House

Take a Tour of Tournament House

Get in the right frame of mind for the January Tournament of Roses Parade with a tour of the Pasadena, California, headquarters. Some 1,500 rose varieties grow outside a 22-room mansion, once owned by the Wrigley family. Free guided tours are held every Thursday through August. Visit *tournamentofroses.com* for more information.

Travel Tips for Nature Lovers

You don't have to be a hard-core adventurer to enjoy the great outdoors. Here's how to get the most open-air fun out of any vacation.

**BY KIRSTEN SWEET
AND STACY TORNIO**

Getting away is about experiencing new places, scenery, climates—and more often than not, that means getting out into nature. We understand that backpacking in Yellowstone, all-day bird-watching in Costa Rica and back-to-back garden tours aren't for everyone. But there are several ways you can have a welcome encounter with nature no matter where you're going. Here are our best tips.

3+ MONTHS OUT

☐ **Research.**
A simple online search for "birds in Las Vegas" or "gardens of Orlando" may turn up surprising results. There's also bound to be an Audubon Society not far from where you're going.

☐ **Set a budget.** Figure out how much you can afford to spend, then set aside some money for your special nature excursion.

☐ **Don't count out big cities.**
City parks make up nearly one-quarter of the area of San Diego, making it a city with lots to do and acre upon acre of green space. A city may be known for its restaurants, museums or nightlife, but it doesn't mean that you can't see birds, flowers or other wildlife there, too.

☐ **Visit city websites.** Most have recreation listings that include parks, walking trails, nature preserves and more. Let them spur your imagination.

☐ **Get to know the local birds.**
If the area is new to you, learn about the birds of the region. Note which species you can expect to see in the season you'll be visiting.

1 MONTH OUT

☐ **Make a schedule.**
If the prime viewing opportunities are at dawn or dusk (as they often are for bird-watching), you'll want to be prepared.

☐ **Check social media for local events.** You'd be hard pressed to find a county park, botanical garden or nature center that isn't on social media. Check Facebook pages and Twitter channels for events planned during your visit.

Know your companions.
Traveling with family? Friends? Get a good read on just how much nature they're up for. See if they'll try at least one outdoor excursion a day with you.

Take a road trip. Even if you're flying to your destination, you'll see more if you rent a car and get off the beaten path at least once.

Consider camping.
You might not be a camper, but try finding a campground or an area with cabins for a short stay. There really is nothing like being surrounded by nature to open your eyes and your mind.

1 WEEK OUT

Make a list. And then check it twice! You don't want to forget any important items like your field guide or binoculars.

Check the weather. The science of forecasting has improved so much that you can get a pretty good idea of conditions 10 to 14 days in advance. While there are no guarantees, it helps to check the outlook to get a rough idea of temperatures and possible storms. On the other hand…

Plan for a range of conditions.
Hot, cold, rainy, windy: You never know, so be prepared for surprises.

Pack layers. No matter where you are, if you're up before the sun, it probably will be chilly. Bring garments you can easily remove as the sun heats up later in the day.

Check eBird. This website is a fantastic resource that lets you easily explore sightings by location. From *ebird.org*, go to the Explore Data tab. There's no better way to see what's being spotted where you are—or where you'll be.

VACATION TIME

Be spontaneous. Keep an eye out wherever you go—you never know when you'll see a wonderful plant or bird. Take time to smell the roses or listen to the warblers.

Find a park.
Look for local, state and national parks and wildlife refuges. Most are free or have reasonable fees.

Make it a game.
If you're traveling with kids (or even if you're not), keep a tally of the different birds or wildlife you see. It'll naturally make you more aware of your surroundings.

Talk to the locals.
Residents of the area will likely have insider tips on what to check out next, so it's worth asking when you're at a park or garden. People are often happy to offer suggestions.

Find an expert.
Talk to the park ranger or an extension employee—people who are paid to be in the know. The folks at garden centers and bird shops can be helpful, too.

Vacation Essentials

Don't forget these basics to enjoy the outdoors on your trip.

Binoculars
Sunscreen
Raincoat
Jacket
Sturdy shoes
Backpack
Camera
Sunglasses

Use a backpack to keep your hands free and to keep your field guide, water, camera and extra layers within easy reach.

homegrown Harvest

Whether you are looking for something easy to grow, or interested in trying your hand at canning, read on. Or try growing a chemical-free garden, planting an area with foods from specific parts of the world, giving back with your gardening know-how, and more.

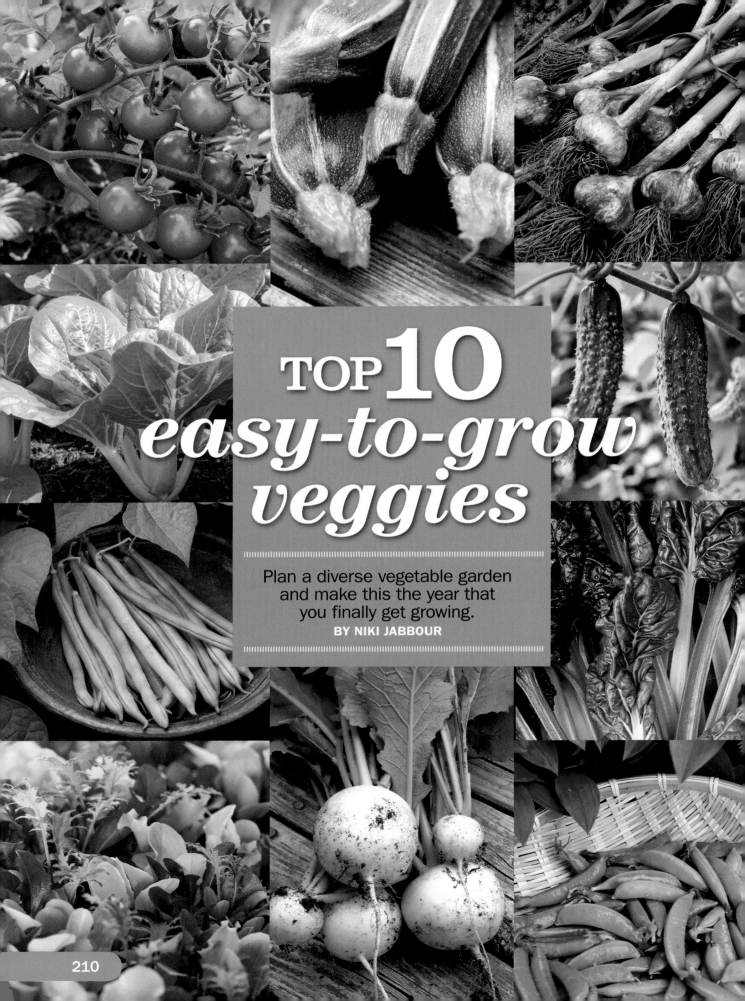

TOP 10
easy-to-grow veggies

Plan a diverse vegetable garden and make this the year that you finally get growing.

BY NIKI JABBOUR

TOP 10

1 BUSH BEANS
2 ASIAN GREENS
3 CHERRY TOMATOES
4 ZUCCHINI
5 SWISS CHARD
6 GARLIC
7 PEAS
8 CUCUMBERS
9 LETTUCE
10 JAPANESE TURNIPS

While a veggie garden isn't a plant-it-and-forget-it endeavor, you can decrease the amount of time and work needed by picking the right vegetables from the beginning.

Good planning will help you figure out how much space and time you can devote to your garden and what types of vegetables you should grow. If you're new to vegetable gardening, start small. As long as your chosen area receives at least eight hours of sunlight a day, a manageable 4x8-ft. bed is big enough for an initial plot. If an inground garden seems daunting, remember that you can also grow most veggies in containers. Just stick with these 10 easy options:

▲ Bush beans

For new gardeners, it doesn't get easier than bush beans. Find a sunny spot with decent soil, press the seeds about an inch into the ground and presto! Within days, you'll have seedlings. Bush beans are ready about 50 days from seeding. Green pods are the norm, but I'm a sucker for yellow and purple varieties, too. Sow together for a rainbow of color!

Growing Tip: For a constant supply of homegrown beans, sow a new row of seeds every two to three weeks, starting in late spring.

▲ Asian greens

Popular at gourmet restaurants, most Asian greens are ready to harvest in just 30 days. To grow, sow foot-wide bands of seed as soon as you can prepare the soil in early spring, and continue to plant fresh seed every few weeks for a nonstop salad garden. Best bets include varieties of mustard, mizuna, bok choy and tatsoi.

Growing Tip: Most greens thrive in the cooler temperatures of spring and fall. A little afternoon shade will extend their harvest into warmer months.

◀ Cherry tomatoes

Cherry tomatoes have a high yield, bearing long chains of delicious fruit. They're also a cinch to grow, thriving in large containers or garden beds. Can't-fail varieties include Black Cherry, Supersweet 100 and Sungold, which all yield a large crop of sweet tomatoes.

Growing Tip: Stake tall or indeterminate varieties of cherry tomatoes to keep plants off the ground and help prevent the spread of soil-borne diseases.

▲ Zucchini

In terms of sheer production, it's hard to top zucchini. One plant can pump out dozens of tender fruit during summer months. Zucchini come in a wealth of colors and shapes with varieties like Zephyr and Eight Ball. Whatever type you choose to grow, harvest young for optimum flavor and texture.

Growing Tip: Zucchini grows best in rich soil, so be sure to add a few shovelfuls of compost before planting.

▲ Swiss chard

Swiss chard is easy to grow, productive and ornamental, making it a great choice for vegetable and flower gardens. For gardeners more interested in yield than beauty, stick to the prolific, but less showy, white-stemmed varieties like Fordhook Giant. Adventurous gardeners will be drawn to the hot hues of Bright Lights, Peppermint and Magenta Sunset.

Growing Tip: If you're looking to pretty up your container garden area, you'll definitely want to add chard. You can't find a better, longer-lasting pop of edible color.

▲ Garlic

If you want a low-maintenance vegetable, look no further than garlic, which practically grows itself! In cool climates, hardneck garlic is the best choice, while those with mild winters should grow softneck garlic. I plant about 500 cloves each autumn, harvesting a bounty of homegrown garlic the following summer.

Growing Tip: After planting, mulch your garlic bed with straw to prevent weeds and hold soil moisture.

▲ Peas

Homegrown peas rarely make it into our house. Instead, we eat our peas straight off the vines, enjoying their crisp, sweet flavor in the middle of the garden. There are three main types of peas: shell, snow and snap. Depending on the variety, they can grow on plants as short as 1 foot or as tall as 6 feet. Peas enjoy cool weather, so sow the seeds in early spring. Then plant again in summer for a fall harvest, too!

Growing Tip: Vining varieties must be staked, but even bush types appreciate some twigs or chicken wire for support.

8

▲ Cucumbers

Cucumbers are produced on either bush or vining plants. Bush varieties have tidy growth and you can easily pop them into containers. Vining types produce long plants that sprawl on the ground unless encouraged to climb a fence or trellis. My favorite cucumber is Lemon, a popular heirloom with delicious, yellow-green oval fruit.

Growing Tip: The secret to bitter-free cucumbers is to supply even moisture. If rain is scarce, water thoroughly, giving plants 1 inch of water per week.

9

▲ Lettuce

If you enjoy daily salads, growing your own will shave serious dollars off your grocery budget. Leaf lettuce is the easiest type of lettuce to grow, with varieties like Black Seeded Simpson, Red Sails and Red Salad Bowl—they're all ready to harvest in just one month! Sow seed directly in pots or in your garden beginning in early spring.

Growing Tip: Start harvesting when the plants are about 3 to 4 inches tall, removing the outer leaves and allowing the inner heart of the plant to keep growing.

10

▲ Japanese turnips

A farmers market favorite, Japanese turnips like Hakurei and Mikado are super speedy vegetables, ready to pull just five weeks from seeding. They also offer a double harvest with their crisp roots and tasty greens. Japanese turnips love the cool weather of spring and autumn, so start sowing in mid-spring and then plant again in late summer.

Growing Tip: Because turnips grow so quickly, plant seed between slower growing crops, like tomatoes.

bonus round

Even if you're a novice gardener, don't be afraid to try new or unfamiliar vegetables.

- **Kohlrabi.** Once you've grown this underappreciated member of the cabbage family, you won't want to be without it. Depending on the variety, the odd, rounded stems will be soft green or bright purple. You can enjoy them raw or cooked.

- **Celeriac.** Also known as celery root, celeriac is a celery cousin that forms a large, knobby root. Use it as a celery substitute in soups, stews and on veggie trays.

- **Quinoa greens.** Typically, quinoa is grown for its edible seeds, but did you know the young plants can also be harvested as a nutritious green? Enjoy them as you would spinach.

- **Dinosaur kale.** This trendy heirloom kale, also known as lacinato kale, is tasty and beautiful with blue-green, puckered leaves and a mature form that resembles a palm tree!

Radish
microgreens

INDOOR PLANTING IN 5 EASY STEPS

1. Select a sunny location—one that gets four to six hours of sunlight a day. A south-facing window is best.

2. Select a proper planting vessel: a shallow plastic tray, a disposable pie plate or a to-go container. Provide adequate drainage by poking small holes in the bottom.

3. Fill with 2 inches of clean potting medium and smooth until level. Scatter seeds and lightly press into soil. Use a packaged mix so the greens will be ready to harvest at the same time or grow a single crop. Spread a fine 1/8-in. layer of soil on top.

4. Keep soil consistently moist by misting from a spray bottle.

5. Snip with scissors when 1 to 2 inches tall. Stagger planting to harvest weekly.

Mini-Me Microgreens
Good things come in small plants.

WHAT ARE THEY? Immature, near-perfect seedlings of your favorite full-grown vegetables and herbs. (Think something between sprouts and baby greens.) Packed with nutrients and flavor, they adorn plates at gourmet restaurants.

HOW DO THEY TASTE? Delicate to intense, sweet to spicy, their flavors resemble what you would expect from the full-grown plant. Foodies and chefs love the array of colors and textures they come in, too.

WHY GROW THEM YOURSELF? Two words: Instant gratification. You're harvesting these little guys when they're only 1½ to 2 inches tall, so you're getting them on your plate a couple of weeks after sowing.

EASY TO GROW? The only way they'd be any easier is if they'd sow themselves. Well, they also need a few inches of clean soil, four to six hours of sunlight and a hit of mist from a spray

bottle every day to keep them happy. Grow them almost anywhere—a windowsill, countertop or container.

HOW DO YOU SERVE THEM? Microgreens are delicate, so eat them raw and within a few days of harvesting. After snipping, gently rinse and pat dry with a paper towel. Top soups and salads, fill sandwiches or use microgreens to garnish appetizers or main dishes.

WHERE DO YOU GET THE SEEDS? Any seed can be grown as a microgreen, but some packaged mixes are suited for sprouting and provide a blend of popular varieties or the plants have similar germination rates.

Micro, but Mighty

Researchers with the University of Maryland College of Agriculture and Natural Resources and the U.S. Department of Agriculture say many microgreens contain four to 40 times more nutrients—vitamins C, E, K and beta carotene—than their mature counterparts.

Good to Grow
If you're just getting started, give one of these a try:

Arugula	Clover
Basil	Cress
Beet	Kale
Broccoli	Lettuce
Cabbage	Peas
Carrot	Radish
Chard	Spinach
Cilantro	Sunflower

Preserving Answers

Before you dive into canning and other food preservation, get an expert's DOs and DON'Ts.

DO sharpen your knives before canning and preserving. A sharp knife will give you a clean cut, wasting less overall.

DON'T spend a lot of money on kitchen gadgets, but do invest in a few key items. For instance, if you're going to be working with cherries, it helps to have a cherry pitter to remove the stones.

DO get locally sourced food for home food preservation. You'll have better results with produce that comes from your local grower, farmers market or backyard garden.

DON'T overfill your jars when canning or freezing. Filling them too full could prevent a good seal

DO reuse canning jars from years past. As long as the jars aren't chipped or scratched, you can keep on using them and passing them down to the next generation of canners. Just buy new lids and bands.

DON'T think you need a lot of extra space to can. Two burners and about a tea towel's worth of space is all it takes to get going.

DO look at other methods for preserving food in addition to canning. Freezing and drying are both great ways to preserve.

DON'T buy old fruit and veggies. Food for canning should be at its freshest—picked no more than a day before processing.

6 WAYS TO PRESERVE FOOD

- Refrigerating
- Freezing
- Canning
- Drying
- Fermenting
- Infusing

garden don'ts

13 garden remedies that aren't true, so

Adding sugar to soil might actually harm tomatoes, not make them sweeter.

STOP DOING THEM!

BY STACY TORNIO

There's no need for "Dear Abby" in the garden. Just go to your gardening friends or neighbors with your plant question or problem, and they're pretty much guaranteed to have an answer.

But how do you know those tried-and-true tips, often passed down from one generation to the next, actually work? Gardeners are great at giving advice, but that doesn't mean you should always follow it.

Authors C.L. Fornari and Jeff Gillman have both written books about garden myths and remedies, so they've heard it all. They're helping us tackle 13 garden myths that are common practice for many. With their tips and advice, backyards across America are going to be much better off.

Myth 1: Make your tomatoes sweeter by adding sugar to the soil.
Save your sugar for making hummingbird feeder solution, instead of sprinkling it over your soil. If you want to grow sweeter tomatoes, look for different tomato varieties intentionally bred to be sweeter.
C.L. says: Sugar can actually stunt the growth of plants, which would be downright tragic when it comes to homegrown tomatoes.

Myth 2: If a plant is wilted or yellow, water it.
It's natural to reach for the watering can when you see a plant wilting or yellowing, but water isn't always the answer. If water is your go-to remedy for droopy or discolored plants, it's time to reconsider.

Jeff says: Unless the soil is dry, there is no need to water. In fact, overwatering is just as likely to be the cause of the problem as not watering enough.

Myth 3: Bury banana peels to give plants, like roses, much-needed potassium.
If your banana peels are going in the garbage anyway, why not put them in your garden? This is one of those myths where you might think it can't really hurt to try, but be sure to keep your expectations in check.

Jeff says: Banana peels do offer potassium, however, burying them will also suck up nitrogen that plants need to grow. As with coffee grounds, the best thing to do with banana peels is to compost them.

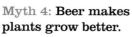

Myth 4: Beer makes plants grow better.
It might be tempting to try, but unless you're getting your information from an actual horticulturalist, it's best to ignore all advice related to pouring liquids other than water onto your plants.

C.L. says: If Mother Nature intended plants to be grown with beer, she would have made Sam Adams pour out of the clouds. Beer may be a refreshing drink at the end of the day, but it's a terrible waste to pour it on a plant.

Myth 5: Don't water plants in the middle of the day, because it will burn them.
Your plants probably won't burn, but this is actually a piece of advice you'll want to follow most of the time. If you must water during the day, it's OK. Keep the water low to the ground at the base of the plant.

C.L. says: Although the best time of day to water plants is in the morning, if a plant is thirsty, then you should water it. Brown spots on leaves are usually caused by leaf-spot fungi, not water and sunlight.

Marigolds aren't a magical solution for pest problems.

Myth 6: Coffee grounds make your soil richer.
You've probably heard of adding coffee grounds to the compost pile or even local coffee shops saving grounds for community gardens. It's not true to a point, but you still need to know what you're doing.
Jeff says: This may be the case for some plants, but others do not respond well. The best place for coffee grounds is the compost pile.

Myth 7: Use tar or varnish to protect newly pruned trees or shrubs.
After you prune trees or shrubs, they tend to look vulnerable and exposed. It's tempting to do anything you can to protect them, but before you reach for that tar or varnish, get a little advice from our experts.

Myth 8: Keep bugs away from your veggie garden by planting marigolds.
There is no scientific evidence showing that marigolds repel bugs. While there are great gardeners who swear by this method, it's not a magical fix. If your garden has pest problems, look into an alternative solution.
C.L. says: Marigolds might not deter harmful insects, but I plant them anyway. As my husband says, "It's tradition!" On the plus side, their petals are edible, they look cheerful and the flowers attract pollinators to the garden.

Jeff says: As a general rule, mothballs don't work. Instead, prune at the end of the winter when diseases are dormant.

Myth 9: Mothballs in the garden will dissuade pests.
Should you be digging deep into attics, closets and garages to pull out the mothballs you find? Probably not. It really won't do your garden much good.
C.L. says: Mothballs are toxic, and who wants to be spreading toxins in the garden?

Myth 10: Support newly planted trees or shrubs with a stake.
Although you may want to give a

Myth 11: Plant a rusty nail to make your hydrangeas blue.
If it were this easy, you'd have gardeners all over the country rummaging through basements and sheds looking for rusty nails. Bottom line is that it's just not going to get you very far. Stick with science if you want to get blue blooms.

C.L. says: I live on Cape Cod where blue hydrangeas are our signature plant, and we know that it's the acidic soil that allows them to develop that outrageously wonderful color— not a rusty nail.

Myth 12: A mixture of dish soap and water can eliminate bad bugs.
Often touted as a natural remedy, it's tempting to take to the garden with a water and soap mixture to get rid of annoying bugs like aphids. While this does have some truth to it, it can also harm plants.
Jeff says: This can work, but too much dish soap might burn the plants, so be careful. Test a small area if you're set on trying this. Even better, use soap made for plants.

young tree some sort of support to reduce the chances of it flopping over, this is only necessary in a few cases.
Jeff says: Extra support may be needed for some floppy specimens, but use stakes as little as possible. It causes the tree to form thinner trunks, and if the wires aren't removed, it can lead to damage from strangulation.

Myth 13: Double your fertilizer for double the results.
The person who first thought of the phrase, "too much of a good thing," could have been talking about garden fertilizer, which can do wonders in the garden, but going overboard is not the best idea.
Jeff says: Doubling the fertilizer is likely to cause fertilizer burn on your plants rather than increase their growth. Follow the instructions on the container.

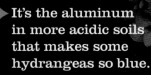

It's the aluminum in more acidic soils that makes some hydrangeas so blue.

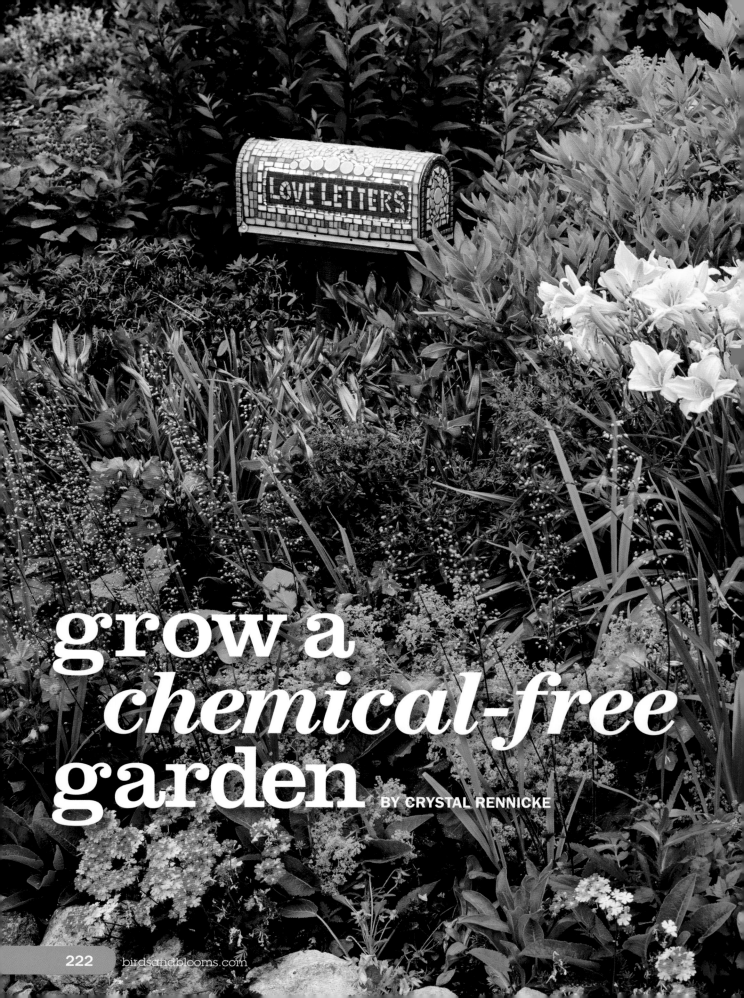

LOVE LETTERS

grow a
chemical-free
garden

BY CRYSTAL RENNICKE

When you go chemical-free, you may need to control weedy and aggressive plants the old-fashioned way—by hand

*W*in the war against weeds and pests without all the harsh chemicals. Yes, it really is possible to have a harmonious yard with a more natural approach.

Why Eliminate Chemicals?

Even if you don't have children or pets, there are plenty of reasons to steer clear of chemicals. For starters, pesticides, fungicides and herbicides don't just kill pests and weeds—they also kill helpful birds and insects. According to the National Audubon Society, an estimated seven million birds die each year because of exposure to lawn pesticides.

Pesticides also come with hidden consequences, like polluting the runoff water that flows into our water systems. A number of lawn pesticides contain carcinogens, which are linked to birth defects, and nervous system, liver and kidney damage.

But if we can all agree that eliminating pesticides from our home gardens is a great idea, how do we go about doing it?

1. Creeping thyme

2. Marjoram

3. Tarragon

4. Rosemary

7. Dill

8. Oregano

9. Fennel

10. Salvia

STEP ONE

Nurture Healthy Plants

The first line of defense in a pesticide-free garden is healthy plants. Pests prey on weak plants, so keep your plants as healthy as possible. Start with the soil. Load it up with as much compost and organic matter as you can. This provides the perfect environment for healthy, strong plants.

"It's all about developing the soil," says Calvin Bey, an organic gardening educator from Fayetteville, Arkansas. "My natural method for eliminating insects and disease in the garden is the development of healthy soil, alive with beneficial microbes and containing a balance of minerals."

Organic mulch will protect your soil and provide a habitat for beneficial predators like ground beetles, centipedes and spiders.

Picking the right plants is important, too. Choose plants that are resistant to disease, native in your area and fit the growing conditions.

"If you grow nutrient-dense produce, the pesticide issue pretty much takes care of itself," Calvin says. "When you get started, you might need to use a little diatomaceous earth and BT (*Bacillus thuringiensis*). These are natural products that can help with specific insects."

STEP TWO

Invite Your Allies

Less than 1 percent of the pest population of a garden can truly be considered pests. Most insects are allies, ready to take on the bad bugs. These unsung garden heroes include:

Pollinators (bees, butterflies and moths). They transfer pollen between the flowers of fruiting plants, fertilizing female flowers, so fruits and seeds develop. They are important to tree crops, berries and veggie crops.

Parasitic wasps and parasitoids (wasps, ants and sawflies). They control garden pests before they become a problem in your garden.

Predators (birds, ladybugs, spiders, damsel bugs, dragonflies, lacewings, ants, ground beetles and praying mantises). They feed on garden pests that get out of hand.

5. Lavender

6. Mexican sunflower

11. Sage

12. Yarrow

13. Mint

PLANTS TO ATTRACT BENEFICIAL INSECTS

1. Creeping thyme
2. Marjoram
3. Tarragon
4. Rosemary
5. Lavender
6. Mexican sunflower
7. Dill
8. Oregano
9. Fennel
10. Salvia
11. Sage
12. Yarrow
13. Mint
14. Catmint

14. Catmint

To encourage these helpful insects to visit your garden, you first have to stop using pesticides. These garden friends can be wiped out when pesticides are used.

Next, plant with insects in mind. Choose colorful, flowering plants to attract bees and parasitoid wasps. Grow a variety of plants at different sizes, including shrubby structural plants, plants with lacy foliage, and herbs for bees and other pollinators. Don't be too tidy with your garden design; a more natural garden will provide shelter and nesting spots for birds and other beneficial insects. Allow some plants to go to seed and some herbs to flower such as dill, cilantro, basil, oregano and thyme.

STEP THREE

Natural Pest Solutions

If you are looking for a solution to a specific problem, try a less toxic product, like insecticidal soaps or horticultural oils. These are helpful in controlling aphids, caterpillars, crickets, fleas, flies and mites. But don't use them if bees are present.

To deter slugs, try placing coffee grounds or copper mesh around your plants. Use strong-scented soap like Irish Spring to deter rabbits and deer. Cayenne pepper works for other critters. Take steps to attract birds like robins, wrens, flycatchers and warblers that feast on insects and control pests, and provide plenty of nesting sites with native shrubs. Ask fellow gardeners or your local extension service for other natural methods for controlling a specific pest or disease.

"Often all you need to do is spend time in the garden," says Erin Riley of the organic garden site, *yourhopegarden.com.* "'The best fertilizer is the shadow of the gardener,' is a common and true saying. You might need to pull some weeds or hand-pick some bugs, but time spent in the garden is time well spent."

Around-the-World Gardens

Pay homage to your ancestry or favorite cuisine with a culturally-themed vegetable garden in your own backyard.

Whether you have a large plot or a small patio garden to work with, fresh veggies and herbs that highlight different countries around the globe are fun and functional.

START SMALL AND BE SELECTIVE
When designing a cultural garden, choose only a few edibles—specifically, the ones you cook with most. You can always add on or switch out plants.

LOCATION, LOCATION, LOCATION
Consider how much sun the proposed site receives in a given day. Most edibles need around eight hours a day to thrive.

INTERMINGLE PLANTS
Edge edibles with ornamentals to keep the look pleasing and pretty. Just consider an ornamental plant's potential growth, so it doesn't end up eventually overshadowing low-growing vegetables and herbs.

GROW UP
Include one vertical grower, which provides interest. Cucumbers, heirloom tomatoes and pole beans are good choices.

CULTURAL GARDEN IDEAS
Each of these themed gardens includes common vegetables either grown in a particular region or used extensively in the local cuisine. Feel free to mix and match to your taste!

French
Ooh la la. A high-style potager (kitchen garden) featuring these favorite French goodies is simply magnifique!

- Alpine strawberry
- Chard
- Chervil
- Culinary lavender
- French green bean
- Garlic
- Leek
- Savory
- White asparagus

Mexican

Cook up the freshest fare around with these must-have ingredients. The number of chili varieties out there is endless—choose a few to spice up your life.

- Chili pepper (jalapeno, poblano, serrano)
- Cilantro
- Epazote
- Heirloom corn
- Heirloom squash (summer and winter)
- Red Mexican bush bean
- Tomatillo

Mediterranean

A garden best suited for temperate climates—hot, dry summers and moist, cool winters. Envision a living tapestry of color and texture.

- Artichoke
- Dwarf eggplant
- Greek oregano
- Marjoram
- Mint
- Onion
- Rosemary
- Sweet pepper
- Thessaloniki tomato
- Zucchini

Dwarf eggplant

Savoy cabbage

Italian

The vegetables and herbs in Italy are as varied as the cuisine.

- Broccoli rabe
- Cipollini onion
- Fava bean
- Fennel
- Heirloom cantaloupe
- Italian parsley
- Roma tomato
- Romaine lettuce
- Savoy cabbage
- Sweet basil

African

Keyhole gardens, which originated in Africa, are great options for hot, dry climates, as they hold in moisture and nutrients. For more information on how to plant a keyhole garden, visit keyholefarm.com.

- African eggplant
- Cabbage
- Corn
- Mustard greens
- Peanuts
- Pumpkin
- Spinach
- Squash
- Sweet potatoes/ yams
- Tomatoes

Asian

These exciting vegetables may be used in stir-fries and salads, or to accompany Chinese dishes. Use fermented cabbage in kimchi.

- Bitter melon
- Bok choy
- Daikon
- Edamame
- Green onion
- Lemongrass
- Napa cabbage
- Snow peas
- Thai basil

Eastern European

Polish, Czech, Slovak, Russian and German cuisines are about more than sausage and pierogies. Whip up a flavorful borscht or cabbage rolls from these offerings.

- Beets
- Cabbage
- Cucumber
- Dill
- Kohlrabi
- Mushroom
- Potato
- Radish
- Turnip

English

Go old school with a four-square garden, which consists of four rectangular plots connected by two intersecting pathways, usually enclosed by a fence with an entry gate.

- Asparagus
- Brussels sprouts
- Carrot
- Cauliflower
- Currant
- English cucumber
- Garden peas

CHECK IT OUT: Cleveland Cultural Gardens

Featuring 31 plantings each inspired by a different ethnic group—Polish, Greek, Italian, German, Hebrew, Irish, Chinese, African-American and Indian, to name a few—the Cleveland Cultural Gardens in Rockefeller Park is a must-stop destination in Ohio. For more information, visit *culturalgardens.org.*

Grow a Row

Help your community by planting a row of vegetables for the hungry.

PLAN

Plant a Row for the Hungry is a program from the national Garden Writers Association and encourages gardeners to plant veggies to donate to food programs all around the country. Learn more and sign up to participate at *gardenwriters.org*.

PLANT

Your involvement can be as simple as adding a row of veggies to your own garden or as extensive as staking out a large growing space with family, friends or co-workers. However you participate, this is an easy way to give back to your community.

GROW

Once you're growing food, the only thing left is to find a local agency to distribute it. Find a participating group through the Garden Writers' site, and then put together a harvest plan.

Easy Harvest

Here are some inexpensive, easy and much-needed items that would be good to grow for this program.

- **POTATOES**
- **LETTUCE**
- **HERBS**
- **CARROTS**
- **PEPPERS**

BY THE NUMBERS

20 million pounds of food have been produced for this program.

1995 was the year Plant a Row for the Hungry began in Anchorage, Alaska.

4 people benefit from every pound of produce donated.

33 million Americans live in households that experience hunger.

84 million households have a yard or garden, so just imagine what a single row from each one could do.

200+ local groups now keep the national program running.

5 years is all it took to reach the first 1 million pounds of donated food.

10 weeks is all you need before planting season to start your own Plant a Row effort in your community.

What kinds of herbs should you grow?

See which plants suit your style

1. WHEN IT COMES TO GARDENING...
■ My backyard is full of plants.
■ I've got a couple of pots on the balcony.
■ I've tried and failed, but teach me more!
■ I'm a total newbie.

2. WHEN IT COMES TO COOKING...
■ I'm the next Julia Child.
■ I love to experiment and throw stuff together.
■ My family tells me I'm a good cook, and they eat whatever I make.
■ I'll cook anything as long as it's six ingredients or fewer.

3. FAVORITE CUISINE?
■ Thai.
■ Middle Eastern.
■ Italian.
■ Mexican.

4. MY TASTES SKEW TOWARD...
■ Spicy and strong.
■ Peppery and sweet.
■ Mild and clean.
■ Anything and everything—I'm not picky.

5. I WANT TO GROW HERBS...
■ Indoors, right on my windowsill.
■ Year-round, inside and out.
■ There's no space in my kitchen—outdoors only.
■ Wait, I can grow them indoors and outdoors?

MOSTLY BLUE.
Experiment with the robust, refreshing flavors of **mint** after you grab it right from your kitchen garden. Use **rosemary** sparingly, but enjoy its strong flavor in stews and sauces, or try flavoring olive oil with it.

MOSTLY RED.
Sage is peppery with a touch of mint. It's great for meats like sausage and beef. Try **thyme** if you're going to experiment with Middle Eastern dishes. It goes well with sage, so see what you can come up with.

MOSTLY YELLOW.
Simple to grow, **basil** and **oregano** are great additions to your meal plan, especially with Italian favorites like pizza and pasta. Try **dill** to amp up summer salads; freeze it if your outdoor garden overproduces.

MOSTLY GREEN.
Some of the best herbs for new gardeners are **dill**, **parsley**, **sage**, **chives** and **cilantro**. The onion flavor of chives makes them suitable for most dishes. And don't forget to add cilantro to your favorite Mexican dishes.

Get the Most from Compost

Our field editors share their tips for composting better and smarter.

1

We take all the leaves from our half-acre, which includes about 10 canopy trees, like oak and maple, and we pile them high in our compost area. After that, we simply dig holes in it every few days when we have uncooked veggies and fruit to add. We use a glass cookie jar by the sink to store kitchen waste.

Marie Higgins
WILLOW GROVE,
PENNSYLVANIA

2

Our small compost bin is where we put all of our kitchen fruit and vegetable scraps as well as coffee grounds. We use a plastic gallon ice cream container to collect the scraps, because it seals well and doesn't attract fruit flies. We also add a lot of the trimmings from our flowers to the compost mix as well.

Ken Wellnitz
DAVENPORT, IOWA

3

My husband and I have become better at collecting all our scraps. We try to have a variety of scrap piles, and make sure they stay moist by watering the piles when we don't have rain. I put all my dirt from last year's baskets and pots in my scrap piles as well.

Barb Lassa
WISCONSIN RAPIDS,
WISCONSIN

4

Add yarrow to the compost pile. It helps speed up the decomposition process and will add potassium, magnesium, calcium, phosphorous and other valuable nutrients to the compost.

Darcy Larum
JANESVILLE,
WISCONSIN

5

I have horses, so I plant everything in a combination of peat moss and composted horse manure, which is a mix of manure, uneaten hay and grass clippings, left to sit in a big pile for a year or two. In rural areas, there are plenty of places giving away horse manure for those without their own horses.

Leda Klein
BYRON, NEW YORK

did you know?

Veggie harvest times vary based on temperature and growing conditions, but here are a few tips to get you started.

45
Snap beans are ready to pick in 45 to 60 days, but don't let the seeds in the pods get too big.

55
Sow carrot seeds in early spring. Plant a new crop every few weeks for a continuous harvest. It'll be about 55 to 80 days until you can take a bite.

85
Chili peppers need a little more time to ripen than bell peppers. Give chili peppers about 85 days and bell peppers about 75 days before picking them.

1
Pick Brussels sprouts when they're about 1 inch in diameter and before the leaves turn yellow, about 90 days after planting.

8
Harvest established asparagus plants in the spring. Cut spears off at the ground when they're as thick as a pencil or about 8 inches tall.

50
Be sure to do some research on the type of cucumbers you're growing. Depending on variety, it can take anywhere from 50 to 100 days for them to be ready for harvest.

4
Take your head of broccoli to the table when it's 4 to 6 inches in diameter. It'll taste best if harvested before buds start to flower, which is typically at 55 to 60 days.

butterflies Unlimited

It's a rare soul who isn't thrilled by the sight of a brilliantly hued butterfly perched atop a flower in the glittering sun. Learn how to spot and attract these tiny fliers as they skip from bloom to bloom in search of nectar.

bring on the *butter*

flies

Butterflying is one of the fastest-growing outdoor hobbies in North America.

BY KENN AND KIMBERLY KAUFMAN

Gulf fritillary on chrysanthemum

Butterflying!

This hobby is parallel to birding. In short, it involves finding, identifying and enjoying the many kinds of butterflies in the wild. It's the perfect activity for anyone who enjoys being outdoors on gorgeous, sunny days—and who doesn't?

Juniper hairstreak on wisteria

A World of Variety and Color

It's no wonder that thousands of people are taking up this pursuit. More than 600 species of butterflies live in the U.S. and Canada, and they come in limitless colors and sizes. To see all these varieties, you would have to travel to beautiful landscapes all over the continent, from mountain meadows in the Rockies to subtropical woods in the Florida Keys or desert canyons in California. Of course, you don't actually have to travel to see butterflies. As with birding, butterflying offers surprises and rewards right in your own backyard.

Identifying Butterflies

With so many kinds out there, it helps to have a good field guide to identify your finds. When you see a butterfly, start by considering the size: Is it large like an eastern tiger swallowtail, small like a spring azure or somewhere in between? Keep in mind that little butterflies don't grow up to be big ones—they are full-grown by the time they go through the pupa stage and emerge as winged adults.

Next, look at wing shape. Are the wing edges irregular like those of an eastern comma? Do they have long "tails" on the hindwing, like a zebra swallowtail? The color pattern of those wings is important as well. Sometimes the best field marks involve minor details of just a few different spots or lines.

Flight action is worth watching, too. The monarch and viceroy butterflies have similar color patterns, but the monarch sails along with its wings held up in a shallow V, while the viceroy makes several quick flaps and then goes into a flat-winged glide.

Some people prefer to go butterflying with a camera, taking pictures of their finds, and then looking them up later. If you do this, be sure to take photos from all angles. Sometimes you need to see the wings from both the top and the underside in order to make the ID.

Eastern tiger
swallowtail on lantana

where to look

Overgrown fields with a variety of wildflowers are always a good place to check for butterflies.

Bronze copper

Checkered white
on butterweed

where to look

Many butterflies are attracted to mud puddles to absorb salts and other chemicals.

Viceroy on Mexican hat

particular areas. For example, the little wood-satyr likes forest edges, the bronze copper lives around marshes and swamps, and the meadow fritillary prefers damp meadows. Some butterflies are almost always found very close to the host plants for their caterpillars: juniper hairstreaks are usually perched on eastern red cedars and other kinds of junipers, while eastern pine elfins are invariably close to pines. If you explore new, natural habitats, you are likely to find new butterflies.

Try Every Season

As long as you have a mild, sunny day, there is no "best" time of year to look for butterflies. In fact, it's good practice to try different months of the year. Some butterflies have long flight seasons, but others are flying for just a few weeks in spring, midsummer or fall. If you go out repeatedly at different seasons, you'll find a distinct mix of species on the wing each time.

Where do butterflies go when you're not seeing them? A few types migrate, but most are permanent residents. When you don't see adult butterflies on the wing, it just means they're going through their other life stage: egg, larva (caterpillar) and pupa. Butterfly eggs are pinhead-size and hard to spot, but searching for the caterpillar and pupa stages can add interest to your time outdoors. However you decide to approach it, butterflying can enhance your enjoyment of the outdoors and your appreciation of a world of small wonders.

The Right Binoculars

Binoculars for watching butterflies? At one time, that wouldn't have made sense. Until recent years, no binoculars would focus any closer than 20 or 30 feet away, too far to be useful for such small creatures. But optics companies have heeded the needs of naturalists, and today you can find binoculars that will focus down to less than five feet, allowing you to see fine details on even the tiniest butterflies without scaring them away. Check the figures for "minimum focusing distance" when shopping for optics. Not only are close-focusing binoculars ideal for watching butterflies and other little things, they'll also give you stunning looks at birds visiting bird feeders right outside your window.

Finding Sunshine

For successful butterflying, you don't have to tough it out in bad weather. In fact, there's no point in going out when it's cold or rainy, because butterflies won't be flying. The best butterfly activity is on warm, sunny days without too much wind. A few kinds will fly on cloudy days, even in the deep shade of the forest, but most like sunshine and they'll stop flying when it's overcast.

To find a good variety of species, it helps to visit a variety of habitats. A few types of butterflies will range far and wide over the countryside, but many are limited to

The Basic Butterfly Groups

- **Swallowtails.** Large butterflies, often with extended "tails" on hindwings.
- **Whites and sulphurs.** Butterflies mostly of open country, usually white, yellow or orange.
- **Blues.** Very small, with weak, fluttering flight. Usually blue on top of wings.
- **Hairstreaks.** Very small, fast-flying. Often have threadlike "tails" on hindwings.
- **Coppers.** Fairly small, mostly in fields and marshes. Usually with some coppery brown markings.
- **Fritillaries, crescents and checkerspots.** Medium to small. Usually orange with intricate pattern of black on top of wings.
- **Brushfooted butterflies.** Our most varied group, large to small, but often very colorful.
- **Satyrs.** Usually some shade of brown. Floppy flight, often in wooded areas.
- **Spreadwing skippers.** Small, with thick body and fast flight. Often some shade of gray, black or white.
- **Grass skippers.** Small, with thick body and fast flight. Usually some shade of orange.

Fritillary on
bee balm

Clouded
sulphur on
butterfly bush

Marine blue
on rock cress

where to look Put out rotting fruit or a sugar-water feeder to attract butterflies to your backyard.

Gardening for Butterflies
Attract more of these fluttering beauties to your backyard with a few simple steps.

GROW HOST PLANTS

We can't stress enough how important it is to have host plants in your garden plan. Native milkweed is important for monarchs, but don't stop there. Passionflower, violet, hollyhock, chokecherry, snapdragon, dill, everlasting and switchgrass are other great host plants.

Great spangled
fritillaries
on milkweed

PLANT NATIVES

Natives are naturally better for birds, bees and butterflies. If you're overwhelmed about where to start, look up a good native plant source in your area. Then ask them what they recommend.

ELIMINATE PESTICIDES

A caterpillar isn't going to make it to the butterfly stage if you're using pesticides in your yard. While it's tempting to have weed-free, green lawns, it's best to say no to all yard chemicals.

KEEP 'EM BLOOMING

Butterflies are active as early as February and as late as November in many areas. (Of course, if you live in a warmer climate, you get an even longer butterfly season.) Offer plants with early and late season bloom times, so butterfly visitors always have something to eat. You can't go wrong with this logic. It works great for attracting beneficial bees, too!

Basic Butterfly Behaviors

Learn some of their common habits so you won't have to wing it in the field.

BY JILL M. STAAKE

These two pipevine swallowtails are mating on American speedwell.

It's such a treat to see butterflies in your backyard. But it seems that almost as quickly as they flit in, they dart off again, leaving you with barely a glimpse. These fascinating fliers, however, have characteristic habits that can help you spot more of them. Here are a few things to look for when you're in butterfly territory.

Basking. Butterflies are ectotherms, which means they rely on external sources for body heat. In the morning, and throughout cooler days, they must spend time in the sun with their wings spread, raising their body temperature to roughly 85 degrees before they can fly. A few minutes of basking in the sunshine raises their temperature as much as 20 degrees above the surrounding air.

Flight patterns. Butterflies have four wings, two on each side of their body. These are connected in such a way that the wings can move independently, allowing a wide variety of flight patterns. Some species soar slowly, with only a few wing flaps, while others seem to dart in every direction at once. Experienced butterfly watchers can often identify a species from a distance just by noting the pattern of its flight.

Eastern tiger swallowtail

Food sources. Most species drink nectar from flowers, but some prefer fruit juices, tree sap and even dung or carrion. Regardless of the source, they feed with their proboscis, which curls up when not in use. Butterflies extend the proboscis into the liquid, drawing it up into the body. A few also have the ability to digest pollen gathered on the proboscis, giving these species longer life spans. Butterflies also need salts

Monarch feeding

and other nutrients, which they get by drinking from puddles or muddy spots, an activity known as puddling.

Mating. Most butterflies have only a few short weeks to mate before they die. A male finds another butterfly of the same species by sight, then determines its sex by flying close to detect chemical pheromones—a process that often makes the insects look like they're dancing around each other in the air. A male and female mate by clasping the ends of their abdomens together, remaining that way for up to 12 hours so the male can be sure no competitor has a chance to fertilize "his" eggs. The female often flies off to continue feeding, which is why you'll sometimes see two butterflies seemingly stuck together as they fly by. In a day or two, the female lays her eggs one at a time on the appropriate host plant by landing and bending her abdomen up to deposit them.

Resting. Butterflies don't exactly sleep, but they do rest, usually with their wings closed. The undersides of their wings are patterned to provide excellent camouflage. This allows them to land and seemingly disappear from sight—a near-perfect way to elude predators.

Monarch caterpillar on milkweed

Eastern tiger swallowtails puddling

TOP 10
plants for
swallowtails

Transform your backyard garden
into a swallowtail paradise
with these flower favorites.
BY JILL M. STAAKE

TOP 10

Every butterfly gardener delights when showy swallowtails make an appearance. These butterflies are some of the largest in the garden, and their colorful wings and soaring flight patterns make them a treat to watch. After working for several years in a butterfly garden in Florida, I've learned which flowers swallowtails seem to gravitate toward the most. Coincidentally, these 10 plants will draw in other butterfly species, too.

▲ Bee balm

MONARDA DIDYMA, ZONES 4 TO 9

Often grown for the minty citrus scent of the leaves, bee balm has striking tubular flowers that swallowtails can't resist. Native to the eastern U.S. and Canada, it doesn't often tolerate the extreme humidity of southern summers, but it thrives everywhere else.

Why we love it: Swallowtails love it, but deer typically stay away, which is always a bonus!

▲ Ironweed

VERNONIA SP., ZONES 5 TO 9

Many native wildflowers are attractive to butterflies, and ironweed is no exception. A late summer bloomer, ironweed sends flower stalks up to 7 feet with fuzzy purple flower clusters at the branched ends. For best flowering, be sure to provide moist soil.

Why we love it: Ironweed is a long bloomer. It lasts well into fall, providing nectar for the last butterflies of the season.

◀ Parsley

PETROSELINUM CRISPUM

Parsley isn't just to garnish your dinner plate! This annual is a favorite host plant for black swallowtail caterpillars. They'll also eat fennel, dill, Queen Anne's lace and other members of the carrot family, but parsley is easy to grow in just about every garden. In the Deep South, provide some shade in the hot summer months.

Why we love it: All parsley, especially the curly varieties, look beautiful as a border in your flower bed or spilling out of a hanging planter.

▲ Coneflower

ECHINACEA PURPUREA, ZONES 3 TO 9

This native wildflower finds its way into every butterfly garden sooner or later. Coneflower is easy to grow and provides masses of tall purple blooms. For best growth, you should divide the clumps every few years. After coneflowers finish blooming, leave seed heads in place for songbirds to enjoy.

Why we love it: The central cone that gives the flower its name makes it easy to see swallowtails (and photograph them) when they land for a meal.

▲ Butterfly weed

ASCLEPIAS TUBEROSA, ZONES 3 TO 9

Butterfly weed is part of the milkweed family, known host plants for monarchs. But the flowers it produces are also attractive to many other kinds of butterflies, including the black swallowtail. This resilient plant is a must-have addition to any garden. It tolerates dry soil and prefers plenty of sunshine.

Why we love it: Butterfly weed doesn't produce as much milk sap as other milkweeds, making it easier to tend for gardeners with sensitive skin.

▲ Pawpaw

ASIMINA TRILOBA, ZONES 5 TO 9

While this shrub can be tricky to grow, it's the host plant for the zebra swallowtail and the best way to draw this exceptionally beautiful butterfly to your yard. The deep root systems make transplanting a bit difficult, so consider starting from seed instead.

Why we love it: In addition to providing food for zebra swallowtail caterpillars, pawpaw produces edible fruit for humans as well.

▲ Joe Pye weed

EUPATORIUM PURPUREUM, ZONES 4 TO 9

This tall, native perennial prefers moist soil where it can stretch up to 9 feet high. The clusters of pink-purple blooms smell faintly of vanilla. Joe Pye weed blooms well into fall, bringing the season's last butterflies to your yard.

Why we love it: Tall blooms give you a chance to observe and photograph visiting butterflies from a different perspective.

8

▲ Citrus
RUTACEAE, ZONES 4 TO 11

Giant swallowtail butterflies lay their eggs on trees in the citrus family, including lemon, lime and orange. This family also includes prickly ash (*Aralia spinosa*) and hoptree (*Ptelea trifoliata*), along with common rue (*Ruta graevolens*). Be careful, though. Almost all of these trees have spiny branches!

Why we love it: Sweetly scented spring blooms and delicious fruit—need we say more?

10

▲ Mystic Spires salvia
SALVIA LONGISPICATA X FARINACEA, ZONES 7 TO 10

Most salvia species are excellent for butterflies, but the tall blue flower spikes of the cultivar, Mystic Spires, are especially suited to large butterflies like swallowtails. Plant in well-drained soil and cut back spent flowers to encourage new growth. If you don't live in a warm region, grow this salvia as an annual instead.

Why we love it: This compact salvia hybrid stands up to heat and humidity all summer long.

9

▲ Pentas
PENTAS LANCEOLATA

The trumpet-shaped blooms that give pentas its common name, starflower, are a draw for many butterflies. Keep this annual well watered, but allow soil to dry slightly between waterings, and deadhead as needed for blooms all summer long.

Why we love it: Tiger swallowtails are especially drawn to the tall red varieties like Butterfly Red. They might even visit the same plants at the same time every day.

more backyard tips for swallowtails

- **PROVIDE A PUDDLE.** Butterflies often drink from mud puddles for water and minerals. Tiger swallowtails will especially appreciate a tiny area in your yard composed of damp soil with small rocks for landing.

- **ADD ROCKS.** A few large flat rocks in a sunny area will invite butterflies to rest and give you great photo opportunities.

- **OFFER SHELTER.** Butterflies need a safe place to rest at night, like a brush pile or tall grasses.

The Value of Milkweed

Give monarchs a lift by adding their host plant to your garden.

BY SALLY ROTH

Look for striped monarch caterpillars like this one on your milkweed plants.

3 Secrets to Growing Milkweed

1. More is better. Milkweed can be surprisingly hard to get started, so overseed to increase your chance of success.

2. Try plants. If you can't get milkweed seeds started, buy plants. Native gardening groups can point you in the right direction for suppliers.

3. Look for variety. With more than 100 species of milkweed, what works for some might not work for others. Don't be afraid to try a few.

The monarch population is at an all-time low. Recent estimates of the monarchs that overwinter in Mexico show their numbers are nearly half of what they were a few years ago. For instance, 60 million monarchs arrived in Mexico in 2012, and this year, it's down to about 33 million.

While there are a number of reasons for this, one of the biggest has to do with something that we gardeners can fix—lack of milkweed.

Evolution of Milkweed

Twenty years ago, common milkweed was exactly that—common as dirt in every field in the vast stretch of the American Midwest and in the East. This was great for monarchs. Since milkweed is their host plant (where adult butterflies lay their eggs), they never had trouble keeping the next generation going.

Asclepias is named for the Greek god of healing

little-known milkweeds

Monarchs will use any milkweed as a host plant, so mix it up with common varieties and these not-so-common options. Also, get to know the native plants in your area, and shop native plant nurseries or online retailers. Here are a few varieties to look for:

Green milkweed (*A. viridiflora*)
Heartleaf milkweed (*A. cordifolia*)
Narrow-leaved milkweed
  (*A. fascicularis*)
Poke milkweed (*A. exaltata*)
Prairie milkweed (*A. sullivantii*)
Purple milkweed (*A. purpurascens*)
Sand milkweed (*A. arenaria*)
Showy milkweed (*A. speciosa*)
Spider milkweed (*A. viridis*)
Tall green milkweed (*A. hirtella*)
Wavy-leaved milkweed
  (*A. amplexicaulis*)
Whorled milkweed (*A. verticillata*)
Woollypod milkweed (*A. eriocarpa*)

Then, Roundup Ready crops showed up—crops that could tolerate the herbicide Roundup without being adversely affected. Unfortunately, one of the plants it killed off was milkweed.

You might not realize just how much milkweed has been affected. Common milkweed still thrives along roadsides today, but it's been wiped out in millions of acres of agricultural fields. This is why researchers are saying monarchs are in danger—the next generation is running out of food and places to lay their eggs.

Lend a Hand
Luckily, lots of gardeners are helping to fill the gap. Growing common milkweed is a cinch. Just plant it, water it and wait for the monarchs. With a fragrance as sweet as honey, it'll attract clouds of nectar-seeking butterflies, as well as egg-laying monarchs. Started from seed, common milkweed can take a few years to flower; started from plants, it'll settle in faster and soon start to spread via running roots.

With more than 100 species of milkweeds (*Asclepias*) native to North America, we could fill our gardens with nothing but these fascinating plants. Only a few species are widely available, though, including bright orange butterfly weed (*A. tuberosa*) and rose-pink swamp milkweed (*A. incarnata*). Recently, common milkweed (*A. syriaca*) has soared in popularity as gardeners become more aware of the monarch butterfly decline.

If you like planting outside of the box, we have some little-known milkweeds to suggest—just check out the list above. So go forth and plant milkweed! The next generation of monarchs needs our help.

Milkweeds have been used medicinally for thousands of years.

Painted lady
Photo by Paul D. Lemke/The Image Finders

Spicebush swallowtail
Finalist in our Backyard Photo Contest
Photo by Harvey Howell

Eastern tiger swallowtail
Finalist in our Backyard Photo Contest
Photo by Lisa Richardson

Giant swallowtail
Finalist in our Backyard Photo Contest
Photo by Sarah Bogden

Common buckeye
Finalist in our Backyard Photo Contest
Photo by Robin Glatfelter

Birdhouse Guidelines
Choose the best dwellings for your backyard birds.

SPECIES	DIMENSIONS	HOLE	PLACEMENT	COLOR	NOTES
Eastern bluebird	5x5x8" h.	1 1/2" centered 6" above floor	5-10' high in the open; sunny area	light earth tones	likes open areas, especially facing a field
Tree swallow	5x5x6" h.	1" centered 4" above floor	5-8' high in the open; 50-100% sun	light earth tones or gray	within 2 miles of pond or lake
Purple martin	multiple apts. 6x6x6" ea. (minimum)	2 1/8" hole 2 1/4" above floor	15-20' high in the open	white	open yard without tall trees; near water
Tufted titmouse	4x4x8" h.	1 1/4"	4-10' high	light earth tones	prefers to live in or near woods
Chickadee	4x4x8" h. or 5x5" base	1 1/8" centered 6" above floor	4-8' high	light earth tones	small tree thicket
Nuthatch	4x4x10" h.	1 1/4" centered 7 1/2" above floor	12-25' high on tree trunk	bark-covered or natural	prefers to live in or near woods
House wren	4x4x8" h. or 4x6" base	1" centered 6" above floor	5-10' high on post or hung in tree	light earth tones or white	prefers lower branches of backyard trees
Northern flicker	7x7x18" h.	2 1/2" centered 14" above floor	8-20' high	light earth tones	put 4" sawdust inside for nesting
Downy woodpecker	4x4x10" h.	1 1/4" centered 7 1/2" above floor	12-25' high on tree trunk	simulate natural cavity	prefers own excavation; provide sawdust
Red-headed woodpecker	6x6x15" h.	2" centered 6-8" above floor	8-20' high on post or tree trunk	simulate natural cavity	needs sawdust for nesting
Wood duck	10x10x24" h.	4x3" elliptical 20" above floor	2-5' high on post over water, or 12-40' high on tree facing water	light earth tones or natural	needs 3-4" of sawdust or shavings for nesting
American kestrel	10x10x24" h.	4x3" elliptical 20" above floor	12-40' high on post or tree trunk	light earth tones or natural	needs open approach on edge of woodlot or in isolated tree
Screech-owl	10x10x24" h.	4x3" elliptical 20" above floor	12-40' high on tree	light earth tones or natural	prefers open woods or edge of woodlot

Note: With the exception of wrens and purple martins, birds do not tolerate swaying birdhouses. Birdhouses should be firmly anchored to a post, a tree or the side of a building.

Source: *Garden Birds of America* by George H. Harrison. Willow Creek Press, 1996.

What's Your Zone?
Plant Hardiness Zone Map

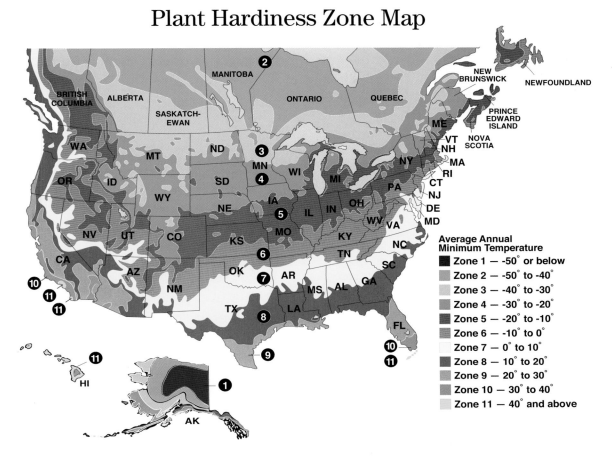

Average Annual Minimum Temperature

Zone 1 — -50° or below
Zone 2 — -50° to -40°
Zone 3 — -40° to -30°
Zone 4 — -30° to -20°
Zone 5 — -20° to -10°
Zone 6 — -10° to 0°
Zone 7 — 0° to 10°
Zone 8 — 10° to 20°
Zone 9 — 20° to 30°
Zone 10 — 30° to 40°
Zone 11 — 40° and above

Plant Heat Zone Map

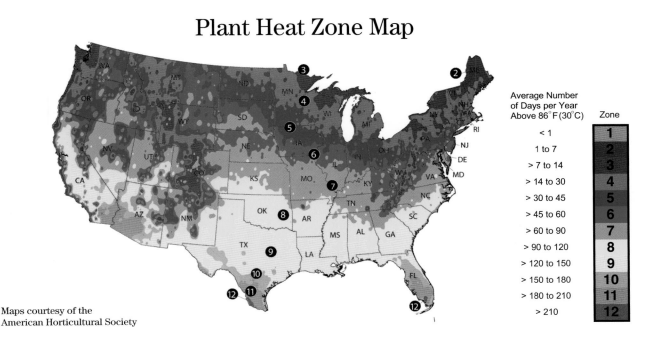

Average Number of Days per Year Above 86°F (30°C) — Zone

Days	Zone
< 1	1
1 to 7	2
> 7 to 14	3
> 14 to 30	4
> 30 to 45	5
> 45 to 60	6
> 60 to 90	7
> 90 to 120	8
> 120 to 150	9
> 150 to 180	10
> 180 to 210	11
> 210	12

Maps courtesy of the
American Horticultural Society

Index

Half the interest of a garden is the constant exercise of the imagination.
-Maria Theresa Earle